A Song for
BRIDGET

PHYLLIS
WHITSELL
with Cathryn Kemp

Mirror Books

Published by Mirror Books,
an imprint of Trinity Mirror plc,
1 Canada Square,
London E14 5AP, England

www.mirrorbooks.com
twitter.com/themirrorbooks

Mirror Books 2018

© Phyllis Whitsell

The rights of Phyllis Whitsell to be identified as the author
of this book has been asserted, in accordance with the Copyright,
Designs and Patents Act 1988.

ISBN 978-1-907324-84-0

First hardback edition

Printed and bound in Great Britain
by CPI Group (UK) Ltd, Croydon, CR0 4YY

Names and personal details have been changed

COVER IMAGES: Topfoto, iStockphoto, Trevillion Images

To both my Mums, Bridget Mary (my birth Mum)
and Mary Bridget (my adoptive Mum).
They had my best interests at heart and, in the end,
I loved them dearly.

CONTENTS

CONTENTS

Cathryn Kemp is an award-winning author, journalist and Sunday Times Bestselling Ghostwriter. Cathryn has written across the full spectrum of the British national press. Cathryn's other books include Coming Clean: Diary of a Painkiller Addict (Piatkus), We Ain't Got No Drink, Pa, and A Fish Supper and a Chippy Smile (both Orion), Jam Butties and a Pan of Scouse (Trapeze) and My Beautiful Struggle (Trapeze).

INTRODUCTION

LETTER TO BRIDGET
February 22, 2018

Dear Mum,

It is 61 years ago to the day that you walked into Father Hudson's Home, an orphanage in Birmingham, and handed me over to the Moral Welfare Officer. I cannot imagine what must have been going through your mind when you gave the warm bundle of your nine-month-old daughter to a stranger, and left with empty arms and a broken heart.

I know that you'd tried so hard to keep me. After giving birth you refused to give me up for adoption, took me home and did the best you could. For a while it looked like you'd tricked fate and stood firm in the face of the authorities who, back then, routinely separated unmarried Catholic Irish girls from their illegitimate babies. We wouldn't stand for it now, but those were different times, brutal times, and it shows me how strong you really were to even try to keep me.

But it wasn't to be.

You were battling terrible odds. Your life had been unbelievably hard; you had terrible experiences growing up in Tipperary, and were left alone and defenceless. You sank into despair, a despair made worse by the comfort you sought from drink and with no chance of a 'normal' happy life. I feel so sad knowing that, underneath the turmoil and drunkenness, was a woman

7

desperately seeking love, desperate to be a mother to her child, but who was simply unable to cope.

Our story began again when I found you, on November 9 1981. I had started my search for you two years earlier at the age of 23. I'd been told by my adoptive parents that you had died, but in my heart I never believed them. So I contacted the orphanage in 1979 and spoke to the very same Moral Welfare Officer, Mary McFadden, who had taken me from your arms all those years ago.

I never told you that I'd tracked you down after all that searching and found, to my delight and terror, that you had lived less than nine miles from where I grew up, five miles from where I worked as a nurse. Neither did I tell you who I was because I feared I might lose you again, that seeing me and experiencing the guilt, shame and terrible sadness at our parting may have sent you fleeing. I just couldn't risk losing you again, so I didn't say a word. I don't know if that was the right thing to do, but it gave me a chance to get to know the real Bridget, not the Tipperary Mary character you had become in the pubs and streets of the city we shared.

When I discovered you were very much alive and living in Balsall Heath, my head spun with shock, not least by the news that at the time you were on probation for causing criminal damage! I knew I had to see you, though it took months before I came up with a plan. But my courage had temporarily deserted me. I decided that it was important to meet you from behind the safety of my district nurse's uniform (though, of course, I wasn't officially your nurse). I'd learnt enough about your fragile state of mind and health, to instinctively know that there was simply no other way. My uniform was the passport to you. It helped me to approach you and show you that, above all else, I was there to help.

I'd been warned what to expect; 'the local drunk', the 'bag lady', Tipperary Mary with a bottle in her hand and a raised fist to the world, and at first you were wary of me, unable to trust a soul, arguing and fighting with a drink or three inside you. Over time, I came to understand so much more about your life, mum. While you never knew that the district nurse who came and tended you for nine years was, in fact, your long-lost daughter, 'Little Phyllis', as you called me.

While I put cream on your cuts and bruises (earned from nights fighting in dodgy pubs), gently combed your matted hair or helped you shower and dress, you talked to me, telling me of the horrors that lay in your past. These things were so hard for me to hear, yet I yearned for your history because it is mine, too. You told me snippets and anecdotes, sometimes laughing, sometimes swearing, your face twisted with painful recollection, and over time I pieced them all together. The fragments of your story became a living, breathing whole over that life-changing nine years, and through that I grew to know and love you, and I vowed to let the world know what it was that had driven you to the life you now led.

I still remember that day when I first met you. I couldn't stop staring. My eyes travelled the contours of your bruised and swollen face, the lines that showed me you'd had a hard life, and I recall the thrill of noticing that we both had the same piercing blue eyes, the same pretty nose. I had never looked like anyone before, as any adopted child or orphan would understand.

But there was something else about your face that was familiar to me, more than just a family resemblance. I later realised with amazement that our paths had crossed very briefly years earlier, when I was working as a nurse in the A&E department of

Dudley hospital and you had been brought in with a head injury after a drunken fight. I had no idea who you were at the time but I remember thinking then, that underneath all the bluster and shouting was a very vulnerable woman.

I listened to you for hours over the years when I cared for you. The only times it was impossible to be with you were when you were roaring drunk. On those days I'd make my excuses and leave, your pale face appearing at the window as I went, as if to say 'come back'. And so I always did. For years I had the privilege of looking after you, the mother I'd never known, the daughter you thought you'd lost.

In remembering our time together, I am still struck by your lack of bitterness, despite the chaos you were born into. You never complained. You shouted, you cried even, but you were never bitter, and I admired you for that. I saw clearly how you drank to numb your pain, and I have never blamed you for that either, nor for giving me up.

I have talked about my own life, growing up as an adopted child, and how I came to find you again, in my book *Finding Tipperary Mary*, but I felt it was now time to tell your life story, leading up to the day when our paths crossed again. While writing I have tried to give you the voice you never had as a child or as a vulnerable young woman. In reliving your life through your words, the stories you told me, and the research I have done here and in Ireland, I have come to understand you better. And the demons that drove you out of Ireland, from which you never seemed able to escape.

You passed away on February 17 2003, but not a day goes by that I don't think of you. I hope that in telling your story I am giving you back some of the dignity stolen from you, and in doing so, creating a legacy in your memory.

I believe you never felt truly loved. So, I will end my letter by saying this: I love you mum. Your spirit is with me. I am sure you are looking down from heaven, watching over me now.

This book is my gift to you.

Love,

Little Phyllis

CHAPTER 1

GROWING UP
January 1938

"Race ye to the steeple!" I shrieked, turning towards the others who were running full pelt, trying to catch me, their hobnail boots clattering on the cobbled streets of Templemore, Ireland.

The wind caught my long blonde locks, and I flew into action, knowing I was faster than all of them, faster even than my elder brother Robert, who was almost a man at 15 years old.

I was just nine, but already wore the worries of the world on my shoulders as my mam's right-hand woman, helping her with chores and looking after my brothers, who were all older than me.

James, 12, or Jimmie as we called him, almost caught up as I climbed over the gate straddling one of the fields that surrounded our small town. I looked around me, taking in the familiar sights. Fields and hills as far as I could see, punctured only with church steeples like ours and villages huddled together. It was the landscape of my birth. I breathed in the frigid air and almost choked with the sheer sharpness of it.

"Can't catch me!" I jeered, laughing, my cheeks flushed from the cold. It was a particularly harsh winter's day yet I was wearing my school frock and only a thin cardigan, which I wrapped around my slight frame. We didn't have the money for luxuries such as winter coats so we all made do with what we had. It was a hard life, yet we knew no different, and everyone was in the same boat. We never had enough food to fill our bellies, and we never had enough clothes to keep us warm, but we got on with life as best we could, never once feeling sorry for ourselves. It was just how it was.

"I'll get ye so I will!" retorted Jimmie, giggling as he leapt over the fence. He was hot on my heels but I knew I would win, I always won our races. I was small, agile and filled with the heady freedom that came after the school bell had rung at the end of each day. Tearing away from the chalkboards and the strict nuns who taught us the sacraments, I couldn't get out of our school fast enough, away from the stifling formalities, the lessons we learnt by rote and the endless hours of catechism, commandments and prayer books. After a day spent with Sisters Benedict, Angelica and Mary Agnes, I needed to breathe, taking in lungfuls of crisp, cold air that sent icy shivers down my back. I relished freedom like an animal released from its cage, with a wild abandonment that belied the sober young lady I was expected to be at home as a 'little mother' with so many tasks to fulfill each day.

Robert had caught up, he grabbed at my cardie but I dodged him, laughing with pure joy. Then Jimmie, whooping, managed to 'tag' Robert and the two of them tumbled to the ground, play-fighting and making a racket.

"I'm goin' to win!" yelled Jimmie.

"Get off me, ye've no chance," blurted Robert.

The pair were always fighting, their rough-and-tumble games sending Mam half crazy most days. My eldest brother, Michael, had already moved away to start a family of his own, at the age of 19, and so it was just me and my two brothers living at home with Mam and our stepfather Patrick.

Michael was a quiet, law-abiding man, considered respectable and upstanding by the community, while Jimmie was the swaggering youngster with golden good looks and a cheek that won him praise rather than rebuke. Jimmie was the apple of Mam's eye, a blond-haired, blue-eyed boy who could do no wrong. He had a sunny nature, was always whistling to himself or playing with his pals. In contrast, Robert, the awkward middle child, was left seething with envy. Robert was more known for his sulks and sullen ways, a 'difficult boy' as Mam often said to him. Robert's personality seemed formed of everything left over from his brothers. He was sly and resentful, prone to telling tales on Jimmie, though it was often rewarded by a slap from Patrick. Robert was tall but puny compared to Jimmie, who shone at sports and could run faster than most boys in the village.

"Get off me, ye bastard or I'll beat ya," shouted Jimmie. It was forbidden by our church to swear and so we enjoyed it all the more when we could get away with doing it!

"Ye'll have the priest onto us!" I laughed, picking up speed. The tall spire of Sacred Heart Roman Catholic Church loomed over us. It was the backdrop to our lives as we lived in the street directly opposite it. The church, and our faith, was the beating heart of our community, the centre of our small world.

We attended mass every Sunday without fail, and on all our Holy Days of Obligation. It was the moral censor and the emotional comforter for all of us. Our faith determined every aspect of our lives, from baptism to holy communion, from birth to marriage to death and everything in between. It was our guiding light, but already I felt the strictures of it. Even as the young girl I was, I felt the rub of its iron rules, the unmovable dogma that dictated how we lived, prayed, behaved and died; but then it was more of a niggle, the kind that most females felt was our lot at that time. I wanted more than anything to feel loved by my family, and mostly I did. I wanted to make Mam and my brothers happy, so I was happy to help out at home though I noticed even at such a young age, that it was to me that the extra chores fell rather than the boisterous boys!

"Can't catch meeee, can't catch me…" I teased as I ran, hiccupping and gasping for air down the tree-lined avenue leading to the church precincts, running my hand along the cold stone walls, past the side entrance, round to the back, only stopping to double over, taking rasping breaths that plumed from my mouth like smoke from the priest's incense.

Holding my sides, my heart hammering in my chest, I panted like a dog as my lungs demanded air. It was Robert who found me first. He stopped a metre or so from me. He didn't appear to be any worse the wear for having run so far.

"Oh Robert, there y'are. I beat ya again! That was grand, but I thought for a minute I'd lost the lot of yer," I grinned, able to breath more easily now. I stood upright.

"What in Our Lady's name are ye staring at?" I giggled, though I registered Robert's intense gaze.

There was a moment's silence.

"Where's Jimmie? He hates losing, especially to a girl," I joked, but the laughter caught in my throat. Robert was looking at me, standing without moving. There was something strange about him, as if he was seeing me for the first time. I felt immediately uncomfortable, but I couldn't figure out why.

"Stop that, Jaysus Robert… Come on, let's go an' find the others." I made to move off but Robert moved faster. Within a stride he was facing me, my back to the wall, standing so close he was almost touching me. All of a sudden I felt the sensation of being trapped. What was he playing at?

"Robert, go on, what are ye doin'? I don't like it, didn't ye hear me?" I tried to shove past him but my brother was a man in all but name and had the strength of one already. In answer to my pleas he stepped forward again and grabbed my wrists, pinning me to the wall. It was cold against my back and I shivered.

"What are ye doin'? Let me go. I need to get back and help Mam with the dinner. Get yer hands off me!" I demanded, feeling suddenly angry. Why did Robert always have to be so, so… intense?

I'd caught him gawking at me a few weeks' previously, his eyes boring into me as I performed some task at home. I was on my knees beside the old tin tub we all bathed in, scrubbing the boys'shirts in readiness for school the next day, when I felt the hairs at the back of my neck rise. I turned automatically and saw Robert. He made no attempt to stop staring. I blushed but shrugged it off, thinking that if he was so idle that he had time to play silly games, he could be washing his own shirts instead.

Obviously I couldn't say anything like that to Robert, or to my mam. I'd have got a clip round the ear for cheek, and extra Hail Marys as penance at confession on Saturday evening. I carried on scrubbing, the oily suds from the cheap soap barely making a difference to the greying clothes, but I felt him there for a good few minutes before he started whistling an out-of-tune song, and wandered off, leaving me feeling like someone had walked on my grave. I'd forgotten about it quickly enough, I had too much to do to spend time fretting over things I didn't understand. And so, I thought no more about it. After all, he was just my brother.

But this was something else. Now he had his hands on me,

pinning me against the wall. This was akin to holding me hostage and I didn't like it one bit. I struggled. "Take yer filthy hands off me, ye devil," I spat at him.

This seemed to break the spell. Robert scowled. He was never a man of many words, and still he didn't speak, instead he bent his head towards me and for a moment I thought he was going to kiss me the way I'd once seen Mam kiss our stepfather.

"Go away, get off me!" I squirmed.

As if touching something hot, Robert recoiled, dropping my wrists and stepping back. He still had the look of strange intensity on his face but there was also confusion there.

I laughed, lightening the moment. "Get away with ye Robert, come on let's find the others."

It worked. Robert hesitated. His demeanour changed yet he was still looking at me with that peculiar leer on his face. The moment evaporated. I took my chance and leapt off like a young gazelle. Free again, but from what this time?

As I ran, I looked back. Robert was still standing there, his face unreadable, still watching me, and I shivered.

Mary Mother of Jaysus, it's cold, I said to myself, but even then I couldn't be sure if that was the only reason for shuddering. Something felt wrong, but I didn't know what it was. The biting wind soon sent me soaring home though, skipping the short distance to our terraced house on the street beside the church.

From the outside it was a brick house in a row of identical buildings, and inside they all pretty much looked the same; with sparse furniture and pride of place given to a small plaster cast of Our Lady and a picture of Christ's Bleeding Heart on the mantelpiece. As I walked through the front door I automatically dipped my fingers into the small font of holy water in the hallway and blessed myself.

Once inside, the house was dark. The range was unlit, and I shivered again. It was bitterly cold and we needed to eat dinner. I tutted. Jimmie was sat looking mournful at the wooden table in the kitchen.

"What's goin' on. Where's me mam?" I asked, peering into the tiny scullery at the back of the house.

"Dunno Biddy, just got here meself." Jimmie was going to say more but he was interrupted by a great wail from upstairs. We looked at each other.

"Mam's havin' the baby!" I squealed, all at once realising why the fire hadn't been lit and why there wasn't a vegetable stew releasing tantalising cooking smells into the dark kitchen.

"The baby! The baby!" Jimmie leapt up. Without a moment's hesitation we raced up the wooden stairs, our boots announcing our presence with their hullabaloo!

At the top of the stairs was Mrs Conroy, our stepfather's mother. She was a fierce looking lady with frizzy brown hair and lived just a couple of doors down from us. To me, Mrs Conroy looked ancient, but she must only have been in her early fifties. Now she stood with her hands placed firmly on her hips looking down at us.

"Now you two won't be disturbing this little baby, yer new sister, will ye?" She chuckled, momentarily barring our way to the door.

"A sister! Yay, a sister!" I shouted, then immediately realised I was already disturbing her with my excited noise, so I dropped my voice to a whisper.

"Can we see her, please Mrs Conroy, can we?" I pleaded. Jimmie looked up at her, his blue eyes big in his pale face.

"Of course you can. I can see ye'll both be as well-behaved as the baby Jesus. Now, don't forget that yer mam has had a hard time birthin' her and she needs peace and quiet."

"Yes, yes, we'll be quieter than Jaysus, we'll be so quiet Mam won't even know we'll be in there."

With a sigh and another guffaw, Mrs Conroy stepped aside and we both tiptoed into Mam's bedroom. Patrick Conroy, 31, our stepfather, was there, sitting next to Mam and looking pleased with himself, which was a rare sight. Patrick was much younger than Mam and a difficult man, even at nine years old I understood that.

My father James Larkin, 26 years older than my mother, married her in 1918 in the church across from our house. He was a farmer who loved the land surrounding us but was cursed with loving drink and smoking tobacco as well. He died suddenly of sclerosis of the liver at the age of 56, in March 1928, just a month after I was conceived.

In my mind's eye I always saw the image of Mam standing at his graveside with her boys Michael, eight, Robert, six, and three-year-old Jimmie around her, and me inside her pregnant tummy. A child's fantasy maybe, but even in my mam's womb I must've felt her loss, must've keened with grief for the death of my real father, a man I was never going to know. I grew up knowing I'd never be my da's little girl, like so many of my friends at school. I watched their daddies collect them, swinging them onto their shoulders or holding hands as their daughters skipped beside them, and yearned for a daddy of my own.

The cruel irony was that my father had longed for a daughter after three boys. I could only imagine the emotional turmoil my mother suffered when she gave birth to me, with my shock of white-blonde hair, knowing that my daddy would never hold me, never see his daughter. I had been baptised on November 14 1928 and even then, it was the Conroy family who had supported Mam, with Patrick's father being one of my sponsors. Only seven months before, my mother had stood in the same church for her husband's funeral. Things must've been starting to unfold with Patrick, as my mam always said he leaned to her and whispered: "Next time you're here, it'll be our weddin' day," yet the pair of them hadn't formally got 'together'.

It must've been a confusing time, and even at nine years old I could sense that Mam had suffered a lot when I was small. I'd been clothed and fed, but my mother's heart must have shut down in her grief and desperation.

Patrick had stepped into my late father's shoes 15 months after I was born, providing Mam with a man in the house to steady her robust family. In those days it was still frowned upon for a woman to bring up a brood on her own, especially a brood of boys. Mam would've felt the pressure of being a single mother and so Patrick from two doors down moved in, but did little else as far as I could see.

I knew that Mam and Patrick had been drawn together through mutual grief. Patrick, who was eight years younger than my mother, had witnessed the death of his brother John. The 19-year-old had been killed after being knocked off his bike by a horse and cart outside the family house. John had hit his head on a stone and died instantly. Patrick had argued with his brother minutes earlier, and it was said that he never got over the guilt, and perhaps that was why he had such fragile moods.

At the same time, my mother was coping alone with four small children and the pair used to sit outside on rare balmy evenings, sharing cider and talking, perhaps, of their struggles. Patrick moved in quickly and we had been a slipshod kind of family ever since. He didn't work, instead he relied on money given to him by his family. Patrick was unable to hold down a job because of his melancholy.

He was dark-haired and brooding, usually. He drank at the pub, came in, ate his dinner and went back out again most nights, but he wasn't cruel or vicious, that, at least, was a blessing. He was a quiet man, prone to dark moods and days spent sitting alone without a fire or gaslight. We had learned to leave him be, to carry on with domestic life when he was in one of his 'doldrums' as Mam put it.

But today he beamed. He pointed to the little bundle being held by my mother who was sitting upright in their bed. The room had the feral, animal smell of the birthing room as we crept in, noting Mam's tired face and feeling happy that, today at least, she was smiling. Mam looked down at the package of blankets she was holding and said: "Come an' meet yer sister Philomena."

I looked up into Mam's face. She was a woman made plain by deprivation and toil who, with a bit of care and attention, could've been pretty. Her body had been formed by child-bearing. Philomena was her fifth child, yet she wasn't an old woman, just 39. Her hair was cut short at the nape of her neck but left in lank brown waves. She never had time to curl it or dress herself up. She wore the same faded apron day in, day out, as all the neighbouring women did, but she was my mam and I loved her with the passion of the child I was.

"Oh Mam, she's a beauty. Can I hold her?" I begged. My mother shook her head.

"When she's a little older, Bridget, ye can take care of her if ye want but she's too tiny now. Why don't ye give her a kiss instead?"

I leaned over and planted a gentle kiss on her soft head, stroking the whisper of dark hairs on her head.

"I'm yer big sister Bridget, but everyone here calls me Biddy. I'm goin' to look after ye and love ye. We'll be special friends and I'll be a little mother to ye, I promise." I sniffed the new baby smell of her and smiled into her cherubic face.

She wasn't going to be fair like the rest of us, she would have Patrick's dark colouring.

"You'll be a beauty, Philomena, I swear ya will," I giggled.

"That's enough now, Bridget, off ye go and light the range. Patrick's gettin' hungry and the children need to eat."

"Ok Mam," I replied, even though I was already questioning why it had to be me who set the fire and chopped the potatoes for our dinner when there were two other boys and a grown man apparently doing nothing!

I clopped down the stairs, my boots knocking on the steps, reaching for Mam's apron that was wildly too big for me. I wound the ties around me several times and made a fist of making a knot, my fingers were now too cold to do it properly.

That'll do, Biddy, let's get the fire lit, it's perishing cold in here... I muttered to myself. I stopped only to look for the thousandth time at the image of Christ over the mantelpiece. He gazed downwards, directing the onlooker's focus to his heart, which was bared and bleeding. We must never forget that we were sinners who would only be saved by the grace of God. I sighed, scooping up the firewood and the remains of yesterday's newspaper, scrabbling about in the apron pockets for the matches.

At least now I had a younger sister to love. The thought cheered me as I rubbed my hands together, bringing the circulation back into them and turned to light the range. I watched as the orange flame caught the edge of the twisted paper, flaring into light and warmth. With a smile I thanked God for the gift of Philomena and set about peeling vegetables for the supper, humming one of my favourite, more uplifting hymns to myself. A new sister, now that was something to be happy about.

CHAPTER 2

A DIFFICULT CHILDHOOD
1940

"Will ye feckin shut up, ya bastards, get out from under me feet or I'll 'ave ye, so I will..." Patrick crashed in through the front door and staggered into the small kitchen lit only by the flame from the range and a gaslight that popped and fizzed.

Mam sat darning the boys' socks, while Robert and Jimmie were fighting yet again. Jimmie held Robert in an armlock, round his throat, while the elder boy struggled, his face contorted. "Tell Jimmie to let off me then. He's the one bein' a bastard." Mam gasped at Robert's language as he mimicked his stepfather's drunken curses.

"Yer a coward, so y'are, a snivellin' coward. Fight back will ye!" laughed Jimmie.

"Yer a littl' bastard, Jaysus Christ get off me!" Robert countered, and this time Patrick rounded on them both.

"Stop yer fuckin' fightin' or I'll have ye both whipped... None of us are fightin' these days – haven't ye seen the papers? Ireland is neutral in the war. Us men don't fight, d'ye hear me?"

It was obvious now that Patrick was the worse for drink, even though it wasn't yet eight o'clock at night. He'd have been in the pub with his pals, discussing the war that raged in Europe, a time we called the 'Emergency'. The war wasn't making much of an impact on our young lives. It all seemed so far away from

Templemore, where we were already living on rations and life's little luxuries were in very short supply indeed.

Patrick stood for a moment, swaying, running his hands through his oily hair that looked black in the gloom.

"Now you two, do ye want to see the back of my fist? Do ye?" Patrick swaggered, raising his clenched fingers in an uncertain way and staring wildly at the boys. The sight was almost comical, and it stopped them both in their tracks.

We all knew that our stepfather, for all his bluster, would never hurt a fly. He was a weak man, more prone to spasms of weeping and despair than violence or anger, yet when he had a drink inside him he thought he was a big man, and he had the nerve to try and prove it.

I could smell trouble.

I put down the cup I was rinsing as I stood at the scullery sink, washing the dishes.

"I'll get ye, ungrateful littl' bastards," slurred Patrick. "Ye think ye are the men of the house, well I'm telling ye now that you're not. I'm the man of this here house. I'm the man and don't ye forget it." With that, Patrick sniffed and rubbed his nose with the back of his hand, a gesture I'd seen Philomena do when she was tired, a gesture so child-like I forgot myself in that moment and sniggered at the thought.

The room suddenly went quiet, except for the intermittent hiccups of the gas light. I looked up and met Patrick's gaze. His eyes were bloodshot, from the drink I guessed, and he looked furious.

"I didn't mean to upset ye Patrick, truly I didn't!" I cried. We never called him Dad or Daddy, I was never even sure if he was married to my mother or whether they just moved in together and got on with it, as many couples did in those days. I don't remember ever going to church for their wedding day, if they had one.

Mam had taken his name years earlier, but this meant nothing, and whenever I asked if they'd married in Sacred Heart Church they both refused to answer, swatting me away like an annoying fly, telling me to "go an' make yerself useful", so I never knew for sure. I guess it was their secret, and it didn't matter to me anyway. Patrick was never like a father to me. He never had a kind word or gesture. He never kissed me on the head or tucked me up in bed at night. There was no tenderness from him, no fatherly concern. He just seemed to be there, living with us, and whatever went on between him and Mam was also a mystery, as there was no visible affection between them, except for the fact that they shared the same bed. I never heard Patrick say nice words to my mother, or comfort her in any way. I thought of him more like an elder brother than a father figure, and mostly kept out of his way, except for tonight.

"Ye laughed at me so ye did, Bridget. I heard ya. I won't have cheek like that in me own house. Jaysus wept, what ingrates ye are.

"I put food on this here table. I look after ye like me own. I'll swing for ye I will, ye deserve it, laughin' at me, ya littl' bitch…" The man, who was solidly built and 6ft tall at least, was as good as his word, and swung for me, raising his right fist and bringing it down in my general direction. I was just 12 years old, but as I said, I was agile, quick as a snake, and I darted out of his way with ease.

Patrick growled: "Come here, I'll show ye who's the man in this house. Get here for yer punishment." My brothers were now standing against the far wall, looking from Patrick to me and back again, unsure what to do. It was Mam who stood up, with an authority I saw rarely from her. Her darning peeled itself off her lap and rolled slowly to the floor as she stood, then walked over to me and planted her wide lumpen body in front of me.

"Now then, Patrick, me darlin', I won't have ye hit Bridget, she's only a girl. I'll deal with her meself," she said, her voice quivering.

"Move out of me way woman! I'm goin' to give that girl a hidin' she won't forget!" Patrick hollered, but even I could see that he was confused by mother's stand. I cringed behind her, waiting for him to shove her roughly out of his way, but instead the heat seemed to have gone from him. He ran a hand through his hair again, a gesture that would forever remind me of him, and said: "Alright, alright." He mumbled and fell into a chair, cursing under his breath.

I looked at Mam in amazement, winking at her, but Mam shook her head almost imperceptibly.

"I'm goin' to me bed, woman. You see that ye deal with her properly or I'll do it meself in the mornin' so I will."

Mam nodded, giving Patrick a wan smile.

"Let me help ye up there, and then I'll bring some supper if ye have a hunger."

Patrick let himself be mollified and I watched this strange pairing between them both. Mam was normally the passive one, the one who took the brunt of his mood swings, and so I had grown up with a passionate desire to soothe and protect her.

Tonight had been different though, and I was left wondering why Mam had suddenly risen up to defend me. I wasn't left thinking for long.

Minutes later, mother shuffled down the stairs, easing her bulk down the narrow staircase and huffing a little, out of breath, as she came back to the kitchen.

"You boys, get yerselves to bed, go on off with ye, I need to speak to Bridget."

I gulped again, the room suddenly feeling sucked of air. I was going to get it now. For an agony of seconds I was left wondering what the punishment would be.

The boys reluctantly moved themselves up to the only other bedroom. I could hear them jostling as they went up the stairs but my attention was now squarely on my mother. I knew she suffered my presence rather than really loved me. I'd never felt the instinctive bond with her that perhaps others such as Jimmie had with their Mammy, and I tried so hard to make her love me by being a good girl, doing the chores she gave me without complaint, and standing up to the big eejit she lived with. Yet at times like this, I could feel the coolness between us, a coolness I never truly understood, so I shuffled my feet, anxious to hear what I would be denied for my cheek.

"I've been meanin' to speak to ye, Bridget. Me and Patrick have been talkin' and we think it's best if ye stay home with me from now on. I can't cope here by meself with the babby an' all the housework so yer goin' to have to leave school."

I stared at my mother. It wasn't entirely unexpected. A couple of my school friends had been forced to do the same, leaving their learning to look after younger siblings at home, helping their Mammys with chores, but I'd never dreamt it would be my turn so soon.

My stomach sank to my boots. Even though I disliked the rigid school timetable, the religious doctrine and the strict nuns, I still had more freedom than I did at home. Walking to school,

I could chatter with friends such as my best friend Kate, and our bosom pals Rosy and Erin, skip along the road together, whisper 'secrets' and make fantastical plans for the future.

During the school day we'd cast glances at each other, screwing up our faces to make one another giggle behind the backs of the strict nuns who were in charge of our moral and educational welfare. Then after lessons, we ran free, playing in the fields and lanes of Templemore until the light faded and we lurched home to help prepare supper or help with the drudgery of domestic life.

I wasn't ready to be stifled at home, kept away from my friends and burdened with a life that surely awaited me as a woman anyway. I knew how it went. You caught the eye of some lad, who asked your parents for your hand, then it was wedding bells, babies and the rest of your life spent washing, cleaning, birthing and praying. I already knew I wanted more from life than that, but it seemed that life had other plans for me.

"Ye want me to stop goin' to school?" I stuttered.

"You heard me Bridget. I need ya here with me to help look after Philomena. It's the way of things."

"But, Mammy, I don't want to leave school."

My mother, who was also called Bridget but at home was always simply 'Mam', or 'Mother', shook her head and looked down at the floor, refusing to catch my pleading gaze.

"It can't be helped. It's just the way things are done, an' ye'd better get used to it because no-one's goin' to cart ye back to school. I've spoken to the nuns, it's all sorted an' ye won't be goin' back there anymore. I need you here at home so that's the end of it." My mother sighed, looked up at the statue of the Virgin Mary and crossed herself.

"It's time for yer prayers now Bridget. I suggest ye pray for forbearance, an' a bit of obedience wouldn't go amiss, an' don't forget to pray for yer sharp tongue to be softened or ye'll get the back of Patrick's hand one of these days, mind my words."

I knew my mother wasn't being unkind. As she said, it was the way of things, but the 'way of things' rubbed sore with me.

I looked over at the statue of Our Lady. It was a small, chalky white figurine that looked over our daily lives. I prayed to her each morning, and each evening, fingering the rosary I'd been given by my mother. I doubted I'd be granted forbearance.

"It's not fair, it's not fair. Mary Mother of Jaysus help me because I don't want to be a little mother, so I don't." The statue sat as still and as pale as the day she was carried lovingly into our ramshackle home. She gave no sign that she'd heard me. Her face was impassive, her smile disinterested, cold, or so it appeared to me. I prayed again, squeezing my eyes shut for emphasis, asking that mine and all our family's sins be forgiven for they must've been many to live like this.

At that moment I heard a snuffle and the first cries from a wakening Philomena.

"Go an' see to her, Bridget. I've got enough to do with my darning," instructed Mam.

I tiptoed up the stairs, past the gruff snores coming from Patrick as he lay in an alcoholic stupor on the bed he shared with Mam. Philomena's tiny arms were flailing from a drawer placed on the floor. She was two years old but still slept in the makeshift wooden cabinet drawer despite being just that bit too big for it. We couldn't afford a crib, and so it had to do.

I lifted her out, cooing as I did so, delighting in the broad smile that spread across her face on seeing me.

"Come here ye littl' darlin', Biddy's here to take care of you," I said in my low sing-song voice, rocking her in my arms. "Now, let me change that clout around yer wee body, it'll be soakin' wet by now. I'll put some cream on and ye'll feel good as new, so ye will," I crooned to my sister, placing her gently on the floor. She yawned, her rosebud mouth widening and I felt a rush of love so strong I might as well have been her mother.

"I'll be leavin' school to look after ye. What d'ye think about that? I'll brush yer hair, and sing you lullabys and make ye the prettiest little girl on the street. I will, Philly, I will. An' when you're older, ye'll steal the hearts of every lad on this street, in the whole of Ireland. You'll be somethin' special, I promise ya."

Philomena looked up at me, her eyes trusting, and it was my turn to sigh. I adjusted the blanket that acted as a mattress in the drawer, unpinned her wet clothing and pulled her wriggling, fat little arms out of their sleeves, holding the pin in my mouth until I'd dressed her in something clean. Carefully, I pinned her back up, and laid her down, kissing her forehead, singing her favourite song very softly to coax her back to sleep. As her eyelids fluttered, I made a mental list of the next day's chores, the reams of washing, scrubbing, and sweeping that lay ahead. Philomena's eyes finally closed and her breathing deepened. I stroked her hair, and looked down at the little girl who was now in my charge, feeling a well of love mixed with a betraying sense of obligation. This was my life now. I really was a 'little mother' to my sister. My carefree schooldays had come to an end.

CHAPTER 3

TRAGIC DISCOVERY
February 6-7, 1944

"Stay still will ye Philomena, I'll make you look as beautiful as the Virgin Mary but I need ye to sit!" I pulled the one hairbrush we owned through my little sister's dark locks, watching the sheen catch the light with a kind of maternal pride.

"I can't believe that it's your First Holy Communion tomorrow, it's a special day for you, so it is, a special day and I want ye to look your best and outshine all of them!"

At that, Philomena giggled. She was a bonny six-year-old, while I felt ancient at the age of 15. Most of Mam's tasks around the house, and especially those caring for my sister, now fell to me, as the drink had also taken hold of our mother. She had always enjoyed a drink, and she had originally grown close to Patrick through evenings spent sharing cider, but in the past couple of years she had turned to the comfort of the sherry bottle more and more, as Patrick's moods deepened and he withdrew from her, and us all.

Mam's life had been a hard one, widowed, bringing up children almost single-handedly, and now living with someone who was depressed. I don't think she meant to drink so much, it was just that over time her need for it grew and grew without any of us noticing, until she couldn't go a day without her sherry, and now mostly spent her days in an alcoholic stupor or too hungover to be of much use to anyone.

Every afternoon I would be sent to the local store in the square to buy a jug of draft sherry for Mam, skipping along the street, careless with the jug that needed filling, though I never dropped it. In those days it was normal to sell alcohol to children. Along the way I'd call out to my pals, sometimes they'd join me on my trip to the liquor store after school, and we'd swap gossip and I'd have a welcome reprieve from my home life. A couple of other girls had also left school to help out at home, and it was perhaps our only chance in each day to behave like the young girls we still were. I didn't feel ashamed of Mam then, though over time that changed as I realised how deep her reliance on the comfort of alcohol really was.

I was officially a 'little mother', yet it didn't bother me as much as I had thought it would. Over time I'd grown to love caring for Philomena. She was the centre of my world, and the person I loved most. We had a bond that went beyond sisters, a deep affection and mutual love that formed the emotional heart of my life.

It was me Philomena turned to with a splinter in her hand or when night terrors woke her. It was me who shushed her back to sleep, who held her trembling body close, who whispered lullabies and sweet words to calm her fears. It was me who washed her in our weekly Friday night bath, who towelled her hair dry afterwards and told stories to while away the evening hours.

It was also me who did the practical jobs like lighting the fire each morning, making porridge or boiling a few left-over potatoes on the range for our scant breakfast. It was me who washed down the wooden floors, scrubbing them with a horse-hair brush and grey suds.

It was me who donned Mam's apron to chop up vegetables and the occasional neck of lamb or scraps of meat for the pot, and who scraped and washed the plates afterwards. Then each night I attended to 18-year-old Jimmie's darning, his socks and shirts needing endless care, alongside 22-year-old Robert's washing, while Mam lolled on the shabby brown sofa in the lounge, occasionally shouting instructions for me to follow, such as fetching her a beer or the evening's newspaper.

"But I can't wait till tomorrow, Biddy, I want to wear me dress now and show it off to everyone." Philomena looked up at me, her eyes pleading, but with the hint of a cheeky grin that undermined her attempt at begging.

"I've ironed your dress so ye can't go touchin' it! I don't want ye creasin' it an' everyone thinkin' ye come from a broken home!" I countered, chuckling at the sight of my little sister's pouting face.

"Pleeeease Biddy, go arn, let me try it on at least. I'll be careful so I will."

I shook my head.

"Ye won't be goin' anywhere in that dress till tomorrow so I won't hear another word, d'ye hear me? Ye'll be the belle of the ball. There won't be a single girl in the ceremony who will be as pretty as you, me darlin'. I'll make sure your dress is perfect."

Philomena planted a kiss on my cheek, and skipped down the stairs as I sat for a moment, soaking in the winter sunlight that poured through our window. My sister and I shared a bed in the same room as our brothers. Goodness only knows how we managed, but to us it was normal, though I was always careful to avoid being alone with Robert in there.

The boys were out the house by 5am to work on the farm, and Philomena and I would be tucked up together long before Robert returned from the pub at night. But I was never comfortable with sleeping in the same room as Robert. It was an instinct, as he never did anything strange in front of Philomena or Jimmie and privacy was something none of us ever really experienced. We all lived in each other's pockets. We were too poor to live any other way.

The boys (except of course our brothers were grown men now and had jobs on the local farmland) slept in a single iron bed in one corner of the small room, while Philomena and I shared the other, and Mam and Patrick had the room at the back of the house. It was accommodation at its most basic and economical. A two-up, two-down terrace with a yard at the back to hang the washing when the weather was fine and an outside lavvy attached to the house with a wooden door. We knew we lived like church mice but so did everyone else and so our poverty never really mattered all that much. We made do every day of our lives and it became our way of living.

Outside the window, the church steeple pierced the sky, reminding me daily where the cogs and wheels of our daily life were turning, where the real centre of our days was. I always had mixed feelings looking at that holy building, a sense of comfort perhaps, but also a tightening in my chest as if I couldn't breathe.

Today the church looked beautiful, and I felt my heart soar. It was a cold morning, yet the sun was unseasonably bright, and it looked like tomorrow would be the same, perfect for Philomena's First Holy Communion. There had been endless practice sessions at the church, and much fussing over finding a white gown for her, though in the end Mrs Conroy had helped by making it, as Mam wasn't in a fit state. I knew that Mam's drinking was becoming common knowledge in the town now. I heard the whispers in the local stores, the sympathetic looks that were cast my way, and with a child's raw intelligence I knew why. I still went out every evening to buy Mam her sherry but I didn't skip any more. I hurried along, not looking left or right, trying to get there and back without catching anyone's eye.

I looked over to see the froth of white fabric hanging on the back of the door. Alongside it on another hanger was a veil, a wisp of netting, and a posy made of artificial flowers. Philomena would have white socks and shoes to complete the look, and I was proud that she would be taking this important step in her life, and amazed that she had reached the age to do it. I remembered changing her soiled clouts and giving her a bottle of milk as if it was yesterday!

Holy Communion was a hugely important ceremony after weeks of catechism classes. It was the point where God's son Jesus merged with each child in an experience that touched on spiritual intimacy, though for Philomena I knew it was also a chance to dress up and enjoy a special day away from our normal routine. I couldn't blame her. I loved seeing her so excited, and the day passed with a chirpier-than-usual house-hold. I relished my jobs, clucking over my half sister like a mother hen. Finally, there was something to celebrate.

Even Patrick had seemed unusually calm, his face reflecting our lighter mood. He had his troubles over the years. Six months earlier he had suffered a breakdown, no doubt brought on by the grief of losing his brother. I thanked God that Philomena was away from home when it happened: Patrick's other brother Daniel and his wife had taken her to the seaside for a few days.

It was a Sunday night, he was drunk and Robert had said

something that riled him. Instead of slouching off he lost his temper and started throwing furniture, smashing one of Mam's plaster saint statues and screaming that he "couldn't take it anymore". Patrick really frightened us that night. So much so that Mam told Jimmie to fetch the doctor.

When he arrived, Patrick was slumped in a corner, weeping and moaning in an alarming way. The doctor took Mam aside and the two had an animated, whispered conversation, at the end of which, Mam ordered me and my brothers up to bed. The next morning, I awoke to find Patrick had disappeared.

"Mam where's he gone?" I asked tentatively.

Mam looked wretched, it was clear to me that she hadn't slept well, if at all.

"They came overnight. Two men who took Patrick to the asylum," said Mam.

I gasped. It was a huge thing to be carted off to the mental hospital, and I felt a shiver go down my spine. The asylums were dreaded, known as brutal places where men and women were apparently treated like beasts in the field. Stripped, left naked and cold, food served with pitchforks, the list of horrors was seemingly endless.

"They'll gossip about this in the town," I added, unnecessarily. That much was obvious.

Mam sighed. "Well, it can't be helped. I can't deal with him here. He needs help and I'll pray every day that he gets it."

With that, the conversation was at an end, but my mind whirred with the knowledge. Patrick would've been taken to the Clonmel District Mental Hospital in South Tipperary. If he was lucky, his stay would be a short one. No-one wanted to end up as a permanent resident in a mental hospital. Even then we knew that 'treatments' were harsh, living conditions filthy and bare. I shuddered. Whatever Patrick had done, and however bad he felt, I wished for his sake he'd be home soon.

My wish came true. Within a couple of weeks, Patrick was back. He seemed quieter and more withdrawn. Mam said to leave him be, and I was glad to do that.

I had some sympathy for my stepfather, though he was prone to screaming abuse or sinking into mighty depressions. I generally bore the brunt of his rages, yet I saw him as a melancholic man, a man who had little to show for himself. He had his struggles, and I knew he was ill and couldn't help it, though many a time I was left stunned and weeping after a verbal attack on me or Mam.

"I'm off to the village to get myself a paper, woman," he said, in Mam's general direction. "Do ye need anythin'?" He glanced pointedly at the cup of sherry in Mam's hand and she nodded, slurring slightly as she answered him. I didn't bother listening. I knew she wanted Patrick to buy her more drink, and I didn't want to feel the familiar sinking sensation in my stomach at the sight of her boozing on the sofa when I felt she should, in truth, be enjoying Philomena's first steps into our Catholic faith. I blamed Patrick for the fact she'd turned to drink in the first place. He introduced her to cider, and did little to recommend himself as a 'good husband' in my eyes. Mam had done everything by herself. Looking at our domestic situation, I saw a man who did little and a mother who had done everything up until now. It was little wonder she turned to drink as her companion and comfort.

Patrick tutted, but he did it with good humour, and I looked up, surprised.

"And don't think I'm goin' to forget ye, Bridget, no I won't, you'll see." And he went off, chuckling to himself and whistling as he shut the front door behind him.

I shrugged, and carried on sewing little white ribbons onto Philomena's white socks. I wanted her to look perfect the next day and Patrick's moods were a mystery to me. I tried not to let them affect my life, and that included highs as well as his frequent lows.

Patrick soon came back, bursting in through the door, with 'treats'.

"Look what I've got for ye, Biddy." Patrick never called me by my nickname, so I looked up again, a puzzled expression on my face.

"It's a cream bun so it is! I knew that'd make ye happy!" Spellbound I looked again.

"For me?" I stuttered. He'd never bought me anything before. This was surely a joke at my expense, but there it was in his hand; a paper bag containing a fat cream bun. I took it cautiously, waiting for the punchline, the laugh and the rough expulsion of the paper bag and its oozing, gooey, luscious contents from my palm, but nothing happened. Instead, Patrick sat down on one of the wooden chairs at the table and grinned, flapping open his paper with the air of a man well contented with his actions.

"Thank you," was all I could say. What had got into him? I wasn't going to wait around to find out why he was behaving the way he was. I decided to escape while I had my chance, so I dashed upstairs, calling to Philomena and in our bedroom we divided the sticky cake into two magnificent pieces and wolfed it down, barely stopping to breathe. I closed my eyes, swirling the thick cream and sugary jam around my mouth. The taste was heavenly. We laughed in delight, even as the last crumbs were swallowed.

That night, Patrick refused the drink Mam offered him, and again, I wondered what was going on. It must be a good thing though, he must be feelin' better if he wasn't drinking, I thought to myself. Philomena was staying overnight at the Conroys and had been happy as a spring lamb to go to her grandparents in preparation for the next morning. It was always a great treat to spend time with them, away from Mam and Patrick, and the Conroys were a blessing for my little sister. I envied her, though I loved the bones of her. She had grandparents who openly cared about her, who were involved in every part of her life, including Holy Communion, and increasingly so with Mam's declining health.

Just past nine o'clock, while I was still tidying away plates and cups, ready for the next morning, Patrick announced he was going to his bed. I looked up again, Patrick was usually up late, sitting by himself in the darkening rooms, thinking whatever thoughts got tangled up in his mind. Again, this was unusual behaviour, but again I took it as a fresh start, a new Patrick who went to bed sober and got up in a better frame of mind.

As he passed me, he stopped and placed his hand on my left shoulder.

I froze, waiting, for what?

My stepfather had never touched me before. In my living memory, I could not recall a single other time that he made physical contact with me though he had threatened to hit me often enough. I was confused, watchful. I waited with all my senses suddenly alert, but his voice was soft when it came.

"Look after your mammy and littl' sister," was all he said. I turned to ask "why?" but he squeezed his grip on me for the briefest second then walked away, his footsteps mounting the stairs slowly, methodically.

* * *

That night I slept fitfully, waking fully at 5am when I heard Robert leave for his job as a farm labourer, like most of the men in our area. I got up, yawning and stretching my arms to the sky. Philomena was still at her grandparents down the street, in preparation for her big day, so I shuffled downstairs, feeling the early-morning chill, wrapping an old dressing gown around me, feeling my bare feet on the cold floor.

Blinking the sleep out of my eyes, I reached the kitchen. The clock was ticking, the ponderous sound filling the quiet room. Mam was waking up from the sofa where she had fallen asleep the night before and I called over to her that I'd bring her a cuppa when the range was lit. I cut the bread to smear with jam for breakfast, humming to myself as I worked.

Call it a sixth sense or female intuition, but despite the apparent normality of the morning, something felt wrong. My hackles rose. Peering around the room, I noticed that the door leading to the toilet that sat at the side of the kitchen was open. It was always closed, for obvious reasons, and instinctively I went towards the door to shut it. *Who's gone an' left it open?* I tutted to myself.

Then I saw the shoes.

Placed neatly at the door to the lavvy were Patrick's only pair of brown shoes.

What are they doin' there? He wasn't drinking last night. That's a strange place to put your shoes... I muttered to myself, reaching for the wooden door, but it wouldn't open. I tried pushing it again but something was thudding against it, stopping it, something that was clearly bulky. I squeezed my head around the door frame, almost touching the animal-like sack that hung heavy and still. Shock hit me like a tidal wave.

I screamed. I screamed with such force that within seconds Mam had blundered into the cold kitchen, and I vaguely remember hearing Jimmie's voice as well.

I stood, frozen to the spot, watching Patrick's ankles sway several inches above the ground. My eyes travelled up his torso, unable to stop gazing at the lifeless form of my stepfather that hung limply, like butcher's meat, a carcass that led directly to Patrick's neck and head. His face lolled to the side, his tongue, which was swollen and blue, bloated by death, as his neck, clearly broken, was hanging from his own belt.

I screamed and kept on screaming.

Everything became a blur. Jimmie pushed me forceably out of the way and I felt the impact of his body but as something very far away. I couldn't stop the horror, which washed over me again and again. A grotesque enchantment had been placed on me. Wherever I looked, I could see the death mask, the corpse of my stepfather.

"MAM! Mammy, mammy, where are ye?" I yelled at last, breaking the spell that kept me like a statue of ice, feeling like a small child again, wanting my mother to hold me, calm me and tell me everything would be ok. I don't know if she embraced me, I recall only the smallest details of that day, the shoes so carefully placed at the entrance to the brick lean-to, Patrick's tongue hanging out like a dog's, the weight of his body against the door. Then there were Gardai, the Irish police, in the house; I guess Jimmie must've run to the Conroys to get help. Then, all of a sudden it seemed, Robert was home, his voice sharp above the din, Mam collapsed on the floor, everyone's faces white, the disturbance, the impact of our stepfather's suicide and the reverberations felt around the neighbourhood.

There was a buzz of activity but I barely noticed. Eventually someone spotted my shock, the trauma that had engulfed me and I was led to my mother, who by now was propped up on the sofa making strange keening noises. I was guided by unknown hands to sit down next to her. I smelt the sour stench of last night's sherry on her breath but I didn't care. I leant into her warm arms and let her hold me. She moved and I had to sit upright again, then a cup was placed to my lips and a scalding liquid was poured down my throat. Sip by sip I finished the brandy, feeling my head starting to unravel, my senses deadening to the shock.

The taste was horrible, but it soothed me, quietened my head, my raw nerves.

For the first time I understood, albeit in a small way, what it was that people got from alcohol; its temporary solace, its heady, welcome relief.

Over the following few days, all the arrangements were handled by the formidable Mrs Conroy and Robert, who already appeared to be assuming the role of man of the house. Philomena managed to attend her Holy Communion but neither Mam nor I went. How could we? All I could see, both in my nightmares and my waking, was the limp sight of Patrick's body, its wobble on the tremulous leather belt strap. I couldn't eat, I couldn't sleep, and in the depths of my distress, even I could see that it was best not to have gone. So, she took her First Communion without me, the first loosening of the ties that bound me so closely to her. I didn't have the heart to tell her myself that I wasn't going to be there, I couldn't bear to see the look of crumpled confusion on her face. How could I not be there on her big day? So I took the coward's way and left it to Mrs Conroy to tell her.

Even though I missed her, I also knew in my heart that it was best for Philomena to stay with the Conroys. They had curled her into their family, containing their own grief of losing their second son at a young age. The loss did not shatter them, it drew them together, and took my Philomena from me. I wasn't to know it, but Philomena was never to come back 'home' from her grandparents. She stayed there, away from the tragedy that had struck our lives, kept safe, but away from me, who loved her best. Yet I didn't want Philomena to see how upset Mam and I were, didn't want her to be contaminated by the event I'd witnessed. She was lucky, she hadn't seen the suicide, and I wanted her kept away from it and its toxic ripples.

The inquest took place first, as Patrick hadn't died from 'natural causes', then the funeral. I stood at the open grave, unable to look at the coffin, unable to face the ghoulish interest of our community. I looked away without shedding tears. My mother was there, held up by two women friends in our street, sagging between them, her face a picture of loss. She'd buried two husbands, I had no idea how that must have felt. She wept, and in doing so she took all my tears, too.

When I opened the Tipperary Times newspaper in the days following the funeral, I saw the headline '38-YEAR-OLD LOCAL MAN HANGS HIMSELF'. My stomach lurched and I ripped it up, feeding it to the hungry flames, unable to face the terrible truth. After that, I felt that Patrick's death had left a kind of trace on me, on us, as like a snail leaves its slime. I don't think our family ever recovered from the suicide, and the scandal it caused in our tight-knit religious community. Even though Patrick was a drinker like Mam, and had suffered bouts of severe depression, the stigma attached to taking his own life was impenetrable. His suffering made his fatal decision understandable, but it was, to our church and our neighbours, a mortal sin.

After being given those first sips of brandy, drink slowly became a bridge for me between lying awake and the sleep I craved. On nights that I felt the loss of Philomena the most, I crept into the larder and helped myself to a little from Mam's jug of sherry. The sweet oblivion it gave me was a welcome relief from my visions of Patrick's demented, dead face.

I would then climb the steps to my empty bed, cradling my cup, willing the alcohol to send me into a sleep without nightmares, a place Patrick couldn't reach, a place where Philomena still lay next to me, her hair coiled on our pillow, her warm feet digging into my side as she slept, and it worked, most of the time.

Was it at that point when my life began to unravel? Was it my stepfather's suicide or the loss of my darling sister that was the trigger for everything that followed? I would never know the answer to those questions, but something changed that day I found Patrick, something came loose inside me and I was never, ever, able to fix it.

CHAPTER 4

LOOKING AFTER MAM
Summer 1947

There's movement, the door standing solid, stubbornly refusing to budge.

There's a thud as the door hits the weight behind it.

Thud. Thud. Thud.

I push and push but nothing happens, just that weight, that sickening mass preventing me from opening it.

Then I see the ankles, swaying slowly like a pendulum, and I feel sick. I feel like I'm going to faint. My eyes see them hovering above the floor but my brain won't register it, won't acknowledge the unnatural nature of this. I want to scream but the sound sticks. Or perhaps it doesn't? There is a yell, a primal echo around the house. Perhaps it is me who is screaming and screaming. Then Patrick's face, ashen in the early morning gloom. That tongue. It has grown in size, swelled into a monstrous appendage dangling from Patrick's mouth, his rigid death mask, his wide-open eyes, his neck stretched as it hangs off a wooden beam, the leather belt wrapped around it.

Patrick's leather belt.

One of the few good things he ever owned.

I try to back off but the door catches my dressing gown and for a moment I am trapped. Fear rushes up inside me like rainwater bubbling up from a blocked drain. I cannot move, instead I am forced into proximity with this spectacle, an unwilling witness to my stepfather's untimely death.

A bad death.

A death by his own hand.

The screams grow louder until they fill every particle of space around me. Their pitch is high, their frequency becoming painful to my ears, yet still, still I scream. All I feel is loss; the deep unanswered yearning for Philomena.

The nightmare ends, as it always does, with a rough shove by unseen hands, forcing me out of the doorway so I crumple to a heap on the kitchen floor. There is silence then, as if I have entered my own bubble, away from the events unfolding around me.

There is a hazy, other-worldly feel and a buzzing in my ears and it is then I realise I am waking.

Slowly the dream changes, swirls away.

Each morning I open my eyes, my heart pounding in my chest, my body slick with sweat. I fumble in my twisted sheets, grasping for air, for the solid bedframe, anything to break the nightmare completely, though breaking it means the sharp realisation that each day I wake up alone, without my sister.

I sit for a few moments, breathing and blinking, waiting for the tremors to die down and my body and mind to reset, come back to the present. I sit on the edge of my iron bedstead, its mattress sagging underneath me and I shiver in the cold of that bleak summer. The thin net curtains are pulled back, I hated them being shut, and I watch the early-morning light reveal the church spire.

I hold on to the holy sight as if the devil himself had chased me through my dreaming. When the urgency, the panting subsides, I stretch my arms, yawning, hoping that this time would be the last, that I wouldn't keep reliving that terrible moment of discovery, yet knowing it would come again, and again, and perhaps forever I would see Patrick's dangling body, and feel the thud, thud, thud on the door.

It is three years since my stepfather hanged himself. In time, the scandal had faded, replaced by other dramas, other lives whispered about in church, clumps of people talking furtively then scattering like frightened birds when the object of their sympathy, pity or outrage appeared.

Three years of watching Mam's health decline, seeing her misery deepen, and knowing there was nothing I could do to help her.

Mam, who had always been a solidly-built woman with a badly-cut bob and tatty clothes, had once been capable of taking care of us. My earliest memories were of her standing at the range cooking, in her ageing apron, her hair wispy around her face, or darning endless holes in the same socks, shirts and trousers that we couldn't afford to replace. She was never outwardly loving towards me, there had always been a stiffness in her manner towards me, an absence that I couldn't put my finger on. But that didn't stop me loving her fiercely and wanting to protect her.

I don't think she ever got over her depression, so recently widowed then giving birth to me, her beloved dead husband's child, and being left to fend for herself and her four children alone. And now she was left alone again.

There were no support services in those days, no benefits except the poor fund each parish doled out. It was a badge of shame to have to ask for one, and I don't recall her ever doing it, it would've been unthinkable, and so Mam did the best she could with the little she had, helped by neighbours and church-goers in our fiercely proud and close community. Our community existed because it helped its own, but it also meant that everyone knew your business and privacy was an unheard-of luxury. It had suited Mam to live in such a communal way, but the death of Patrick changed things.

Slowly we began to isolate ourselves.

Mam grew ill as her drinking and smoking increased. She was only 49 years old but looked at least a decade older. Her heart was failing her, according to the local doctor, and she had asthma exacerbated by the endless cigarettes she rolled. She walked rarely, and when she did she walked like a stooped, frail, elderly woman.

By day, she sat on the sofa sipping sherry and smoking her fags, and by night she passed out where she lay, snoring, her head lolling on the back of the grubby sofa while I did my best to clear up the detritus of cigarette ends and empty cups that surrounded her. I would whisk a raw egg yolk into her sherry, to try and build up her strength and she'd respond with a cry of "What the feck have ye put in me drink, Bridget?", though she'd never refuse it.

Her weight increased and the little she had been able to do to keep herself tidy and as smart as she could, disappeared. She lost all interest in us, in the world, and even stopped her daily trip to Mass, becoming more and more housebound as the months and years passed.

Each Sunday, Robert and I would hoik her out of the chair, smooth down the wrinkled folds of her dress and brush her hair before walking her to the church.

We timed it so that we were the last to arrive, as I couldn't bear the stares of the other churchgoers, their obvious, saccharine pity.

After the ceremony, we would be the first to leave, half

carrying her, half walking her back home to her sofa. It broke my heart to see her like that, but what could anyone do? I knew that alongside my concern for her, I was also feeling a less acceptable emotion. I knew that part of the reason I hurried her to and from church was because, deep-down, I was becoming ashamed of her. Her obvious inability to recover herself, the clarity of her descent into depression, the dishevelled look of her, all these things provoked a terrible shame in me, a feeling I hated myself for, but which I could never quite conquer.

I saw her through other people's eyes now.

I looked at her large, formless shape, her shabby brown coat and straggly hair and wished she would find the strength to fight the darkness that devoured her. I watched her fill her cup with sherry and light yet another fag and I hated her for giving up. She had me. She had Philomena. We still needed her, yet she had simply disappeared into her grief and deep down I knew she would never come back to us.

I started to hate her, and so the work I had to do to try and clean her, shuffle her to the lavvy, brush her hair and wipe her face, all revolted me. Isn't that awful? I started to pity my mammy like everyone else in our street. I hated myself for feeling that way, and yet I was caught, trapped by necessity and hardship into caring for her, though I willed her to find the love she must have felt, for Philomena at least, and to make that her strength, to rise up again, put on her own apron, carry on despite the tragedy meted out to us. But she didn't, and I knew she wouldn't, and I was struggling, though I loved her with my heart and soul.

"Robert, I'd like a word, if ye don't mind," I said tentatively one evening. My brother had come in from his day working the fields, eaten the stew I'd cooked and was preparing to sit back and roll a cigarette. I didn't want to disturb his nightly ritual and certainly didn't want to engage with him, especially to ask for something, but I couldn't stop myself – I knew we needed to do something about our mam.

"What is it, Biddy?" he growled, not looking at all like he wanted to speak. I was wary of him. My hackles instinctively rose every time he walked through the door. His drinking had increased since Patrick's death and it was clear he had fallen in with a bad crowd. Always an angry man, Robert's outbursts had become wilder, violent even, and by now he was feared locally as a man you didn't mess with.

Well, it was my turn to face him.

We needed help to care for Mam.

I needed help in caring for Mam. I was doing all the household jobs and looking after her as well. I was 18 years old, and I wanted more from my life than the drudgery and boredom I woke to each morning.

I cleared my throat, my pulse beating in my neck.

"I want to ask if ye'll consider getting in someone for Mam. She needs a proper nurse or someone from the village to care for her now."

Robert's face was impassive, for a moment I wondered if he hadn't heard me.

"Robert, did ye hear me?" I stuttered. "I'd like a woman from the village to help me out. It wouldn't cost much, and now you're earnin' good money at the farm I thought – I thought I'd ask ye…"

My voice trailed off. Robert's face closed into a menacing sneer.

I'm goin' to regret I ever said anythin'… I thought to myself, my insides turning to ice, my bowels churning.

Robert took his time. He knew he made people scared, and I think he enjoyed that power. He spat something onto the floor and eventually his eyes rose to meet mine. I blinked again, feeling my heart fluttering. I swallowed but it seemed to get caught in my throat.

"Now see here, sister. I don't want anyone in this village to know what's goin' on in my house, d'ye hear me? I don't want any busybodies gossipin' or talkin' about what isn't theirs to know."

"But, I need help with her, Robert, it won't be for long, just until she's back on her feet." I pleaded.

Robert drew in a long breath.

Suddenly he stood up. He thumped his right fist on the table, scattering the tobacco from his roll-up. I watched the black curled flakes spread across the wooden surface. It was easier than catching Robert's eye.

Now, with a low snarl he spoke.

"Are ye stupid Biddy? Are ye thick in the head? I'm tellin' ye that what goes on in this house stays in this house. There'll be no *helper*," he spat the word, "while I'm head of this house. D'ye hear me, sister, I say 'No'. No strangers in this house. That's my last word."

Instinctively I backed towards the wall. Robert's face was grim, his eyes blazing. I prayed he would calm down, forget I ever said anything. Robert had assumed the role of father figure in the house, meaning his word was law. I say the words father figure loosely, more a despot, sitting on his arse, being fed and having his clothes washed and dried for him each day, while my life disappeared under the drudgery.

But it wasn't just the unfairness of Robert's new position and the authority it gave him that frightened me; no, it was more than that. I sensed he was watching me with an even keener gaze these days as I blossomed into a young woman.

I had grown up sensing that his gaze was a peculiar one, which left me unsettled and wondering what he meant by it. I felt his eyes on me and it didn't feel like brotherly affection, it felt like something else, something darker.

One Friday evening, I decided to have a soak in the tin bath. Robert was out at the pub after his week's work and I was alone, except for Mam who was dozing in the lounge.

Jimmie had recently chosen to sleep at the farm where he worked as a casual labourer – preferring to keep away from Robert, and perhaps Mam as well. It was hard seeing my family disintegrate further, and unsettling to be left alone with Robert.

I missed Jimmie. He was always kind to me when he still lived here, would pick me a small flower on his way back from the fields, would joke with me, and give me an affectionate hug or a pretend clip round the ear. When he told me he was leaving as well, I wept for myself as much as for missing him. Philomena had left me, Mam had turned to drink and now my favourite brother had gone. I felt lonely – and more than a little nervous about sharing a house with just Robert for male company. He had moved into the back bedroom that had formerly been Mam and Patrick's. Nothing on earth would induce me to go in there, convinced that one day I might see the ghost of Patrick, lying in his bed as if suffering from the turmoil in his head. I stayed in the front room, which I'd once shared with my sister and brothers, all alone, while Mam snored on the sofa.

Robert's wages were only just enough to cover our rent and food, and often he would take himself to the pub, leaving me hunting for scraps or forced into borrowing a hunk of gritty bread from one of our neighbours.

I never knew if Jimmie sent money home via Mam or Robert, but he was the sort that would do the right thing, and Mam always had money for her sherry.

I poured kettle after kettle of piping hot water into the tin bath, sighing as I eased my aching body under the warm embrace of the water. Even though I was a girl in my first flush of womanhood, my body felt like that of a charlady, sore from the hours spent on my knees scrubbing, lifting buckets of water to slosh on our steps or out in the yard. The sheer pleasure of sinking into the heat made me close my eyes, my thoughts blank, concentrating on the physical sensation.

Just then I heard a sniff.

My senses became alert.

Had Philomena popped round?

Was Mam up on her feet?

Should I go to her?

I turned my face round.

The kitchen door had been shut but it appeared someone had silently eased it open. I looked again and saw Robert's face. He was peering round the doorframe, watching me. He made no attempt to hide what he was doing, though he had begun quietly enough.

"What are ye doin'?" I stumbled over my words in confusion.

"Ha, nothing, don't ye go imagining things, Biddy. I'll leave ye to it."

Robert's voice strained with a kind of laughter. What was going on?

With a whistle, my brother moved away, pulling the door to. This time it creaked.

He had been very careful to open it noiselessly before.

How long had he been there?

Had he seen me undress?

Had he watched me slide my body into the water?

I blushed, the pleasure of that moment evaporating like the heat from the bath. I shivered, unable to think clearly.

Why was Robert, my brother, watching me?

Why did he stare so?

I recalled other times I'd caught him watching me, his face flushed yet seemingly unembarrassed. He would never look away when I caught him. It was me who blushed and turned first, feeling a prickling sense of shame – for what? Robert and his attention confused me. Once when I was changing my dress I looked up suddenly and saw him standing on the landing looking at me with a kind of hunger in his eyes. I shut my door, said nothing, but my instincts told me to be careful, to avoid him as much as I could.

I knew how men looked at women when they wanted them. I wasn't daft. I saw the courting couples, the boys eagerly chasing the girls they fancied, teasing them, trying to hold their hands. I knew how it was when a man stared at a woman like that, so why would a brother do it to his sister? I shuddered.

The bath was spoiled, the moment ruined. I looked back to check he wasn't there, and when satisfied that this time he really had gone, I got out quickly, grabbing for the towel that hung limp and grey by the mantelpiece, and rubbed myself down, all the while my eyes darting to the door. I half expected him to burst in, but nothing happened. When finally I was dressed, my hair piled on my head, dripping down my neck, my clothes not quite fitting properly as I'd thrown them on in a hurry, I went into the parlour, looking around for him.

He had gone. His cap was missing so he must have gone out.

That at least was a relief.

I hadn't been able to forget those troubling feelings that time. And now, standing in front of him in the kitchen, I regretted raising the issue of Mam's care. I didn't want to bring myself to his attention any more than I had to.

"I see, you're right, Robert. I can see it wouldn't be right to bring anyone else in. I'll forget I ever said anything. Of course I want to be lookin' after our mammy, no-one else would do it right anyway." I smiled a thin smile, hoping Robert would back down.

He grunted then nodded.

"I'm off to play darts with the boys. I won't be back til late," was all he said. Picking up his cloth cap, jangling the coins in his pocket, he left the house, that tuneless whistle I'll always associate with him following in his wake.

I sat down, suddenly exhausted by the effort of my life, washed over with a mixture of relief, and something else, sadness I think. I wished as fervently as I could that things would get better. The clock ticked. The sound suddenly felt like it had trapped me here. I jumped up, throwing off the apron. I grabbed a single penny from Mam's purse which was always left on the mantelpiece and I ran down the road, up and across the precincts of Sacred Heart Church.

I crossed myself as I entered, sidling up to the ornately carved pews, breathing deeply, the vaulted ceiling soaring above me. I looked down the aisle to the altar, bathed in light from the stained-glass windows surrounding it. Stepping to the left, I slid the coin into the box and picked a candle, lighting it from the stub of another and pressing it firmly into position. Closing my eyes, I prayed with as much passion as I could muster that I would leave Templemore. I wasn't proud of longing to leave my birthplace, my family and home, but there it was. I yearned for a life away from its confines, from caring for Mam, from side-stepping Robert, from the endless chores that filled my days. The candle bobbed and flared in the semi-darkness of the church entrance and I stepped outside into the overcast summer's day.

At that moment, an old school friend walked up the avenue leading to the entrance. I'd avoided my friends for so long that at first I didn't know what to say, but my delight at the sight of a friendly face overcame the shame over Mam that had forced me to withdraw from girls of my own age.

"Kate! I haven't seen you in an age!" I smiled, genuinely pleased to see her. She had arrived just at the right time. Kate was a slim girl with a shock of red hair, freckles and the palest skin. She grinned at me.

"Biddy! I can't believe it's you, Jaysus I haven't seen ye fer weeks, holed up in that house like a slave!" Kate shivered as she spoke, wrapping her russet-coloured cardigan around her. "Jaysus it's freezin' an' it's meant to be the feckin' summer!"

We both grimaced. That year, 1947, had been a cold one from the start. We'd had a harsh winter of blizzards and Arctic storms that left many places cut off underneath several feet of snow. Food and fuel crises had beset southern Ireland due to wartime shortages and rationing, which was still in force, and rainstorms were so fierce that entire fields had been flooded. We were all scared that Ireland would see another famine as it was clear many harvests would fail that year, but we had to keep on living.

"So, Biddy, ye'll never guess the news, but there's a funfair coming. Ye've got to come, say ya will, go on…"

Perhaps my prayers had been answered, or at least listened to.

The funfair came once a year to Templemore and it was a huge event that everyone enjoyed, but I hadn't been able to go for several years. It would mean a break from normal life for a day, and that was a minor miracle in itself!

"I'd love to come, so I would. Thank ye Kate, yes I'll come. Blast it, my mammy will cope without me for one day!" I giggled, pulling my arm through Kate's and off we walked, our heels clacking on the road and chattering 19 to the dozen, unaware that everything was about to change for me.

CHAPTER 5

FALLING IN LOVE
August 1947

Staring at myself in our small, cracked mirror I felt a thrill of happiness run through me. My hair, which I'd put in rags to curl overnight, had been released and brushed so it glowed in the morning light. It fell around my shoulders in luxuriant waves, and I smiled at my reflection.

Leaning in, I saw a young woman of 19 with blonde hair and startling blue eyes. I didn't see the worn-down charlady, the 'little mother' I had got used to thinking I was. Instead there was someone quite different: a woman with a capacity for fun and laughter, who relished the thought of a few hours' freedom, and a whole future ahead of her. Turning away, I saw my new red dress hanging on the doorframe. My brother Jimmie had given me the money on one of his visits so I could buy a new frock especially for the occasion.

He'd arrived one evening after a short summer shift in the fields. He walked into the house with his customary whistle and twirled me round the kitchen, remarking how grown up I was and what a beauty I'd make. I'd giggled, enjoying the craik, but at that moment Robert walked in from work, and the room seemed almost to darken at the sight of him.

"Well, I'll be seeing ya, Biddy," said Jimmie quickly. "I jest wanted to give ye a littl' money for something to treat yerself to,

I'll be off now… though I want to see the dress when ye've bought it, mind. I want to tell all my friends to keep their hands off my sister!"

I laughed openly at that, despite Robert's scowl, his promise of a simmering kind of menace, and before Robert could say a word, I'd pocketed the money and returned to the business of cooking tea.

And so there it was, a tea dress made of thick red cotton with a bow at the wide collar and a skirt that whispered around my thighs as I walked. I was so proud of it. I felt like a 'proper' young lady wearing it. I got up and ran my hands down the dress, delighting in the soft fabric, hardly believing it was mine, and even though the day was drizzling with a few breaks for wan sunlight to shine through, I felt lit up - like a fairytale princess about to embark on an exciting adventure.

"Bridget, won't ye come an' sort me out, I've got myself in a spot of bother here." Mam's voice carried up the stairs. I sighed but nothing could squash the feeling I had of impending happiness at the fair.

"Coming Mam, just a minute I'll be there shortly," I yelled, pulling off my nightie and replacing it with my only slip, a rather faded pink thing that must've been almost glamorous once, and then my new dress. The actual dress wasn't new, of course. I'd picked it up at the market. It was secondhand but you could hardly tell, except for a small stain on the back hem. I took a last look at myself in the mirror and holding it at an angle so I could see myself better.

"Ye'll do!" I laughed to myself, then skipped down the stairs taking two at a time, my stockinged feet padding lightly on the wooden steps.

"I'm comin' Mammy, don't ye go worryin' yourself, I'm

here for ye," I sang as I went.

Once in the lounge I found Mam in a crumpled heap on the floor.

"Ah ye've tried to get up to use the lavvy yourself haven't ye? Don't ya know that I'm here to help? Ye mustn't do it yourself, ye could get hurt and we can't have that, no we can't." I stooped over and, with a heave, managed to get Mam back on her feet and together we shuffled to the toilet.

I thought again about how sad it was that Mam had never recovered her strength after Patrick hanged himself, and how over the years her movements had become slower, her drinking and grief weighing heavily upon her. I pitied her. I could see she didn't want to be this way. Many nights she spoke to me, telling me she was in 'a bad way, Bridget, a bad, bad way', but there seemed to be nothing any of us could do to make her stop her self-destructive drinking or her smoking, which was wrecking her lungs and making her cough all day and night.

Philomena, now a pretty nine-year-old girl, visited most days with her nan, Mrs Conroy, but she didn't stay long, except to spend time with me. I always dropped my chores to see her, my love for her still exceeding every other part of my life. I hated living apart, but I also hated her seeing Mam the way she was and so I knew it was a sensible decision to keep her with her grandparents. I missed her though, and every time she kissed me on my cheek and hugged me close before she left, my heart broke afresh.

When she first lived with her grandparents, she would ask me when she would be coming home again. "Soon, soon," I would say, kissing her on the head so she couldn't see my eyes. "But I can't get to sleep without you,' said Philomena once, and I thought my heart would burst. I wanted to tell her that I missed her more than she could ever know, that I was reduced to drinking sherry every night in order to stand a chance of sleeping. But I didn't say any of that. When I could finally speak without betraying my true feelings, I said, "Sure, there must be plenty of room in the bed now without my big feet," and I tickled her until she was breathless with giggles.

After a while, she stopped asking when she would come home and that made me as sad as I was glad. Philomena loved her nan, who was kind to her but it wasn't the same as being with her own sister – at least that's what I told myself. On her visits with Mrs Conroy, Philomena and I would always have a good chat about this and that, the story she had just written – she had a vivid imagination and stories poured out of her – or which of her friends she liked best, or what her wedding dress would look like. I was always looking for signs of unhappiness but there were none. She was a happy little girl and had adjusted well to her new life with her kindly grandparents.

I don't really know what Philomena made of her mother. On her regular visits to our house, she would always pop her head in to say hello to her mammy who languished on the sofa and then, duty done, would scurry away to be with me. Philomena still called her Mammy, but she had never really known her, as a mother, or a person. And now that person was lost to alcohol and her own despair.

"What's wrong with Mammy?" Philomena once asked.

"She feels a bit sad and tired," I replied, at a loss to know what to say for the best. How do you begin to tell a young girl that her mammy is such a slave to the drink that nothing, not even her own children, were more important to her than a glass of sherry. "She's not well Philomena."

"Is that why she always smells funny, like Christmas?"

"Yes Philomena, yes it is."

Mam always seemed to perk up a bit whenever her youngest daughter visited. It was as if, somewhere in that fug of drunken despair, she tried to rally herself so that Philomena wouldn't see the full horror of what she had become. Mam's semblance of good behaviour would be tested today. My day out to the funfair would be the first time I had left her in someone else's care, but I knew she would be fine with the solidly reassuring presence of no-nonsense Mrs Conroy.

"Now then, Mam, Philomena is coming over today to sit with ye while I'm out. She'll be bringing her nan with her so ye'll have to be on your best behaviour. Don't ye go takin' too much of the drink before they arrive, mind, or they won't stay long." As I spoke I cleaned Mam, and brought her back to the sofa. I'd lain out a shapeless brown dress for her to wear and so together we struggled as I pulled off her old one, careful not to show my disgust at the sour smell of it, and helped her into the new one. I set about brushing her hair, fussing over her while she sat patiently, like a small child being dressed. By the time I'd finished, there was a rap at the door and our neighbours, Mrs Conroy and my darling sister, walked in.

Philomena was a beauty. Each time I saw her pale skin and long dark hair I took a breath. She would grow up to be something special, I was sure of that.

"Now look, here's Philly! Come on Mammy, I bet ye can't wait to find out her news." I ran over to my sister and embraced her with a huge smile and several big kisses.

"Look at ye, you're growin' so beautiful, every day more and more like an angel, don't ye think Mam?" I didn't wait for a response. For once I wasn't desperate to spend time with my sister. I could see through the open front door that Kate was outside and waiting for me. Robert was away for the weekend with his darts team, and so I was gloriously untethered, too.

"I must go, ye have fun!" I sang as I darted out of the door. Kate and I locked arms and started to walk towards the field that was hosting the funfair. We were excited, high on life and keen to squeeze every ounce of joy out of the day ahead.

I'd even got a few pence over from buying the dress so had some spending money, a rare luxury indeed! As we walked we talked, our voices carrying with elation, giggling with the sheer intoxication of being together on our way to the greatest social event of the year.

Local boys and young men drifted by, some in packs, some in pairs like us, and they wolf-whistled us, calling out ribald comments or praising our combined beauty.

We pretended not to notice, huddling our heads together and laughing all the more. At the gate, a Romany traveller held out his hat for the entrance fee of a penny. We stood there, batting our eyelashes like Hollywood film stars until the sweet-faced youth, who couldn't have been more than 17, waved us in, our pennies still in our pocket and a free afternoon enjoying whichever rides we wanted.

I couldn't believe our luck.

Everywhere we looked there were flashing lights, groups of youths, the girls all together, the boys in their own gangs. We recognised many of them from our school and church. Gaudy signs hung from each ride entrance, here the waltzer, there the rollercoaster, and we gazed around, taking in the sights and sounds, the whirring electrical pulsing, the bells tooting, it was like a magical land to us.

"Well, I don't know about you, Biddy, but I'm hungry already. Let's spend that penny we saved on some candyfloss, shall we? I can't remember the last time I ate it, can you?" Kate's face shone with pleasure, and I shook my head.

"It must've been years. Golly, years and years. So, let's not waste another minute. I can see the queue, it's not too long, come on." I tugged at Kate's arm and we tripped over to the candyfloss stall, our heels sinking into the muddy grass. The weather had let up a bit, long enough for us to enjoy ourselves I hoped, but I can't honestly say it was like a summer's day, what with the looming clouds and the slight chill. We didn't care though, we were free for one whole day, and that was worth rubies to us. Kate normally spent her Saturdays working at the grocery store in the centre of the village, and this was as much a treat for her.

We joined the queue and stood gossiping, when two young men sidled up, standing behind us. I turned to glance at them, being nosy about who was next to us, and was struck instantly by the tallest, most handsome man I'd ever seen in my life. I think I actually gasped.

"What's with ye, Biddy?" Kate laughed. She had spotted my reaction, and I guess the young man had, too, as he turned to me smiling while I blushed scarlet and cast my eyes down to the floor. They didn't stay there long though. It was like a spell, drawing me to his face, a moth to a flame, and the moment that changed everything for me.

"Ach won't ye stop your daydreamin'." I turned in confusion. The candyfloss seller was holding out a huge pink cloud of sugar to me, and I felt suddenly disorientated. I blinked, trying to get my head together, and fumbled in my purse for the penny to pay him, muttering my apologies, when all of a sudden there was a voice like melting honey.

"No, let me. I'll treat ye." I turned again and this time met the stranger's eyes without blushing. My throat felt constricted though, and I could barely whisper a 'thank ye' before the golden-haired man reached over and, chuckling, handed me the sweet.

"I don't know what's wrong with me. I'm Bridget, but my friends call me Biddy…" My voice trailed off as I took in his blue eyes, a piercing ice blue, and strong jawline, his athletic-looking frame with his smart shirt, freshly starched collars and smart trousers.

"I'm Kate, don't mind my friend Biddy, she doesn't get out much!" laughed Kate, sticking out her right hand.

"I'm Bill, and this is my mate Paddy, pleased to meet ye both," answered the man, taking Kate's hand and giving it a firm handshake.

"Would ye mind, Kate, if me and your pal *Biddy* (Bill put extra emphasis on my name as if curling something delicious around his mouth, which made me redden again) paired up today, went on a few rides like?" Bill's face was earnest. He had impeccable manners and a lightness to him that I felt myself responding to.

What's got into ye, Biddy? I asked myself, *you're actin' like a littl' girl! He's just a man like all the others…* and yet, deep down, I knew he wasn't. I knew, even then, that something extraordinary was going to happen.

"Course ye can! Go an' enjoy yourselves, but make sure ye take care of her, mind. I won't have her mam onto me for handin' her to strange men." Kate appeared to be joking, but she squeezed my hand as if to say 'ok with you?' and I nodded, feeling that my speech had somehow stalled under some kind of sorcery.

I cast Bill a shy look, nodded again and Bill turned, holding out his hand for me to hold, and without thinking, without even the slightest hesitation, I slipped my hand into his as if it was the most natural act in the world.

Everything my faith and my family had taught me told me that this was wrong.

Only 'loose' girls, held hands with strangers, walked with them in public, yet despite a lifetime of being told I had to be pure, virginal, without a stain on my character in order for a man to take me as his wife, I felt the peculiar weight of those expectations gently lift, as if they were utterly meaningless, and this was exactly what I was meant to be doing.

The afternoon became one I would cherish in my thoughts for a long time afterwards. I began to relax as Bill chatted away to me, disarming me with his kindness, his care for my opinion and wellbeing. Every time we got on a ride he'd wipe the seat for me with his handkerchief. Every time I pulled out my purse to pay, protesting that I hadn't contributed, he stopped me by shaking his head and smiling, melting my resistance yet further. That afternoon I felt like the princess I'd seen in my mirror. We went on ride after ride, shrieking with fear as the rollercoaster rattled over its metal arches, sitting close on the waltzer, our legs touching, my heart in my mouth as it whirled and whistled round and round.

I was giddy, but it wasn't the rides that left me so exhilarated.

"Come on, Biddy, I'll win ye a prize so I will," exclaimed Bill, pulling me towards one of the stalls. I was laughing, breathless with the romance of it all.

If I never see him again, I'll always remember today... I thought to myself as I watched him from under my lashes. He had a fake gun and was shooting at a line of cut-out frogs.

"Bingo! I've won, Biddy, see that, I did it!" I clapped my hands and smiled over at him, hardly able to believe that this gorgeous man was winning a prize for me... for *me*!

I'd never had a man court me like this before. And I'd certainly never felt treated for the sake of it. This was an entirely new experience and all the more thrilling for it.

"Which prize shall I get ye?" chuckled Bill, before his eye caught something towards the back of the stall.

"I'll have that, yes that one..." He grabbed whatever it was that he'd won and turned to me, both hands behind his back.

"Now, hold out your left hand for me, no your left one." I frowned, unsure what he was playing at.

"Just humour me, Biddy, I've got the perfect present for ye, so I have."

I nodded, smiling at his gentle persistence. I held out my left hand. I noticed my fingers were shaking slightly. Before I could say anything, Bill grabbed my hand and with his other had glided something onto my ring finger. I looked down. There winking at me in cheap plastic gilt was a pink ring with a fake diamond. I gasped, and this time Bill definitely heard me. He chuckled and with a slight of his hand, raised up my chin so my eyes were staring into his.

"One day, Biddy, I promise ye that I'll make an honest woman of ye. You're the girl for me, of that I'm sure," he murmured and bent forwards, touching his lips to mine. I smelled his hair oil, the Brylcreem all the young men used, and his cheap cologne mixed with a fresh, manly smell. Without a thought, my lips responded to him and for a moment nothing else existed. The fair slipped away, the crowds melted into nothingness. There was just me and Bill and our kiss.

He stopped, moved back, still staring into my eyes.

"We don't want to cause a scandal…"

"No, no we don't," I stammered, my heart beating like a drum.

For a moment I felt unnerved, as if life would never be the same again after that kiss, my very first.

Bill put his arm around me and we walked off together, his step all the more jaunty for our intimacy, or so it seemed to me. He kept up his banter, insisting I would be 'Mrs Ryan' one day, and we'd have seven children.

"Seven!" I gasped in mock outrage, to which he'd giggled, "Oh yes, Mrs Ryan, we'll have seven children and we'll live on a great farm together with no-one else to spoil it, an' one of our babies will be called Philomena."

I'd told him about my sister, and how much she meant to me, while Bill said he was an only child of 20 years old. He'd left school at the age of 14 like most people did, and immediately got work on a farm, which he enjoyed.

We talked about our lives, that afternoon, and even our hopes and dreams. We both wanted marriage, children if God willed it, and to move away from the small communities we'd grown up in. Bill was from out-of-town which was why I'd never seen him before. He could only get to Templemore once every two weeks as it would take him that long to save up his labourer wages to get the bus over to see me. We were already making plans for the future. I could scarcely believe the turn my life had taken in one short afternoon!

Before long it was time to say goodbye. We met Kate who had spent a not-so-romantic afternoon with Bill's pal. They seemed quite happy to say goodbye to each other, but when it came for Bill and me to part, we both lingered as long as we could.

"Ach see the lovebirds won't ye. Have ye made weddin' plans yet?" teased Kate, grabbing my arm.

"Perhaps we have," retorted Bill, grinning.

"I'll see ye soon, Biddy." He grabbed my left hand and raised it to his lips before saying softly, "Soon, I hope, soon." With that he sauntered off alongside Paddy, glancing back over his shoulder to wink at me, while I stood transfixed, watching his easy gait as he walked off to find his bus home.

"Now, what in Our Lady's name is that?" Kate held up my left hand.

"Oh it's nothing, just a joke that's all." I blushed a livid red and pulled the plastic ring off my finger.

"Oh it's *nothing* is it? Well don't ye go gettin' yourself in trouble. He's a handsome man, and even a good Catholic girl like you couldn't be blamed for fallin' for his charms." I hit Kate playfully for that and started to run home. It was getting late and I knew Mrs Conroy wouldn't thank me if she couldn't get supper on her table in time for her army of sons, and my sister.

"Wait for me," shouted Kate indignantly, and we both sprinted home as fast as our heels would let us.

That night I didn't take a cup of sherry to bed with me as I had so often since the trauma of Patrick's suicide, and the loss of Philomena to the Conroys. I stole upstairs with my plastic ring clutched in my hand and settled down under the covers, shivering with the cold but feeling less lonely than I had in years. It had started to rain again and the pitter-patter made a soothing sound against the tiled roof.

I lay against my pillow, holding the ring, turning it round and round in my palm, amazed at the events of the day. Would I ever see Bill again? Would he be as good as his word and come to visit me in two weeks? I didn't know. I didn't know if he was a charmer who made a play for all the girls, or whether he was the real deal, whether his ardour really had been for me and me alone, and whether his jest about marrying me one day was just a bit of harmless banter, or whether this wonderful man might actually be my Prince Charming after all. I had no other option but to wait, and the thought of waiting felt delicious. Having something to actually wait for – now that was a miracle! Suddenly I felt exhausted. I slipped into sleep, still clutching the ring, smiling to myself as the warm glow of my first romance settled upon me. I couldn't remember a happier day in my life. I sank into slumber, hoping I'd dream about the romantic stranger who had made such an impression on me.

CHAPTER 6

LIVING IN FEAR
Autumn 1948

"Come on, beautiful, I'm taking ya for a picnic." Bill swooped in for a kiss, making me swerve him by ducking my head and stepping lightly out of the way.

"Don't ye go ruining my reputation, Bill," I giggled, but despite my laughter I was deadly serious. Being seen with a man was bad enough, kissing him in broad daylight was positively heathen behaviour, and I shuddered to think what might happen if anyone saw us, even though we'd been courting for more than a year.

"I won't be letting ye kiss me here, Bill, and you know it. Jaysus wept I had a hard enough time off my brother Robert after one of his pals saw us kissing at the fair – and that was more than a year ago! I don't want Robert upset again." My voice lost its hilarity. Robert had indeed given me a hard time over that stolen kiss at the funfair. That night, the first time I met my sweetheart Bill, I'd skipped home on cloud nine, my head full to bursting with the events of that day, the fair stranger who'd stolen my heart so completely that even then I couldn't imagine what my life had been like before I met him.

I'd headed up to bed with no thoughts of the consoling sherry jug that night. I slept well, and without the nightmares that haunted me, for the first time in years and awoke with a smile on my face.

But happiness didn't last long.

I clattered down to make breakfast for Robert and Mam but stopped short when I saw my brother standing glowering in the kitchen.

"So what did ye get up to yesterday, Biddy?" he sneered. My bubble burst abruptly. I stood looking at him, feeling suddenly guilty, but for what I wasn't sure – yet.

"Ye were seen acting like a... like a prostitute with a man from out of the village.

Don't bother denying it, Biddy, my mate from the farm saw ye."

I gulped.

"I wasn't behaving like a prostitute, don't say things like that, Robert." I could hear the note of pleading in my voice and I despised myself for it. I resented the boundaries I had to live within as a woman, the strict 'moral' codes dictating my behaviour and deep down I knew I would never truly apologise for my moment of freedom.

Yet I heard myself say, wearily: "I'm sorry Robert. It happened before I knew it, I got carried away." I hung my head. I was in no mood for Robert's temper that morning and I knew the fastest way to cool his anger was to act as meek and mild as I could, though that stung, too.

"I don't want people about these parts talking about us, d'ye hear me? I don't want my sister laughed at as a loose woman. Change your ways, Biddy, or it'll be worse for ye."

I heard that as a threat. If I didn't squash down every part of me that was vital and alive, then it would go badly for me. Perhaps I should've challenged him.

Perhaps I should've asked him straight, what would he do if I transgressed again? But I didn't want to spoil my memories, the lightness that had settled on me, the glow from the day before, and so I didn't. Instead I hung my head still further and whispered "Sorry, I see now what I did was wrong." The words stuck in my throat, making me want to retch.

When I'd told Bill about that on our first 'proper' date two weeks later, he'd laughed but with a hard-sounding edge. He'd reassured me that whenever I was with him I'd be safe, but we both knew what he couldn't do was keep me safe at home.

From then on we made sure we gave Robert no cause for concern, and for a surprisingly long time we seemed to 'get away' with seeing each other. We courted respectably, no public kisses, no holding hands, just sweet moments spent together, walking through the landscape that framed my town. Normally I would've been cowed by Robert's temper and would probably have ended the relationship in fear, but my new-found courage from the thrill of someone like golden-haired Bill wanting me, me, made me fearless. We did everything we could to avoid Robert, choosing to walk away from the town, choosing to sit and eat a picnic far from the neighbourhood gossips, yet I knew none of this would fool my brother for long. And now, Bill was trying to get me into trouble again.

"Alright, my good Catholic girl, I won't be trying anything on, not until we're away from the town anyway." He chuckled, throwing his arm around my shoulder and whistling as we walked.

Every two weeks I'd see Bill when he made the trip over on the bus. Neither of us had much money, but it didn't matter. We'd go for walks, make a picnic to share or idle away afternoons exploring the fields that stretched as far as the eye could see.

As time went on, our passion only increased, though I was still a virgin and intended to stay that way until Bill's ring was on my finger.

I sighed as I leant my head against his shoulder.

"What's bothering my princess now?' he said with mock seriousness. We'd turned out of Templemore, and at that moment, Bill looked around then pulled me behind a tree.

"Tell me everythin', Biddy, my Biddy," he said, as he stroked my hair off my face and gazed intently into my eyes.

"Ach well, we'd have a lot less trouble if we were wed," I said, stoutly. I never felt I had to tone down my opinions with Bill. If anything, he loved me being outspoken and showing my true self, the self that yearned for more from life, the self that yearned for him, for our passion.

"Don't ye go worryin' about that, Biddy, it won't be long now but I still haven't the money to make ye an honest woman." He grinned and before I could stop him, he kissed me, a long, lingering kiss that made my head dizzy and my legs feel like jelly.

I felt lost in him, and it was a heady sensation.

We finished kissing and I blinked as I looked at him. Bill was staring at me as if he wanted to eat me up. I felt shaky. I knew we couldn't go any further with our intimacies, but I also knew that we both wanted to. I changed the subject abruptly.

"So, what are we eatin' on this picnic anyway?" I teased, slipping my hand into Bill's and sighing with happiness. Dragging him away from the tree, we cantered off into the sloping fields and woodlands.

"Pie! We'll be eatin' some of me mam's pie and I swiped a bottle of ale from me pa so that'll keep us going," shouted Bill, swinging me around and making me even giddier.

"Pie! That sounds grand, so it does!" I laughed, feeling all at once wild, free and happy. The sun shone golden on the trees that were changing colour, their russets and reds shining in the swooning Autumn sunshine. I revelled in the country of my birth, it was a glorious land, though I'd never gone more than a few miles from Templemore. Every season, even winter, produced such beauty, and now that I had Bill's love, it seemed even more spellbinding.

"We will wed, Biddy, I promise ye," smiled Bill.

I looked over at him. He had plonked himself down on the grass, spreading his coat out for me to sit on even though there was a distinct chill in the air.

"You're the girl for me. It's you I love, Biddy. We'll be together forever, I promise ye."

My heart was sore with longing for him. "You're the man for me, Bill. I'll love ye till the day I die," I replied, tears springing suddenly to my eyes.

"When I've made enough to pay for the weddin' and enough to keep ye, we'll walk down the aisle together. Can ye wait for me, Biddy, can ye?"

Bill leaned over to me. I'd sat down on his coat, my legs to one side, holding my skirt over my knees for modesty. His hand stroked my face, my throat, my neck. I gasped as he pulled me in again to kiss me, sinking back onto the ground so we were lying together, embracing as if we were truly man and wife.

I wanted more. I wanted to be with him properly as his wife, but I also knew that pre-marital sex was forbidden by the church.

"Please God don't let us wait too long," I whispered to Bill, who burst into laughter.

"Pie, it's time for pie!" He reached over for the wicker basket he had carried with us. I was shaking with desire, and so I took a moment to compose myself, watching as Bill lifted the pastry, wrapped in a muslin cloth, out of the basket.

With a knife brought from his mam's kitchen, he sliced the

thick crust, revealing the pink ham and clear jelly inside.

"That looks delicious, so it does. I hope ye won't be expectin' a pie like that every night when I'm you're wife," I giggled.

"Of course I will," Bill jested, "and I'll expect my dinner on the table the minute I walk in from the fields. Ye'll be a good wife to me, won't ye Biddy?"

I pushed him away, snorting with laughter: "Only if ye'll be a good husband to me!"

At that, Bill roared with laughter and planted a kiss on my forehead.

"I've never met anyone like ya, Biddy. It was my lucky star that shone that day at the fair."

"And mine…" I murmured, biting into the pastry and looking, almost with disbelief, at the handsome man who was my sweetheart.

Later that day, much later, we brushed off the crumbs from our clothes and packed up what was left of our feast.

"I hate havin' to go. I hate havin' to leave ye looking after your mam and that brother of yours," said Bill, helping me up to my feet.

My legs felt stiff from sitting on cold ground, despite the coat, and I took a moment to stamp them on the grass.

"Ach, I don't know what to tell ye. There's no one else who can look after Mam except me. Who else could do it? I don't mind it, I really don't. She's my mother and I like knowing she's clean and fed.

"As for Robert…well, there's nothing I can do about him. As long as I keep out of his way I should be alright…" That part I didn't really believe, but I didn't want Bill going home worrying about me for the next two weeks.

"It'll be grand. Anyway, we'll set up our own home one day

and I won't have to worry about my brother any more, and I'll still be able to look after Mam. She could even live with us, who knows?"

Bill nodded. He knew I took my responsibility with Mam seriously. Even though I'd never felt particularly cared-for by her as a child, I couldn't see her suffer.

We walked back towards the bus stop in silence. It was always like this when Bill left. Neither of us felt able to speak. We hated saying goodbye.

"I'll leave ye here, Bill, I don't want anyone seeing me being too friendly with ye…" I said.

Bill put down the basket and pulled me into a hug, whispering, "Keep yourself safe, Biddy. I'll be back soon. I love ye, so I do."

I smiled, breathing in his warm, masculine scent as he held me.

"I love you too. Goodbye Bill."

I walked off, looking round to wave at him, watching his easy gait as he walked away, doffing his cap to me as if he was a squire and I a lady. I tutted under my breath. His confidence dazzled me, made me wonder what he could possibly see in me.

His whistling becoming more and more faint as he walked. I sighed. It was back to normality for me. I just hoped I'd timed it so that Robert had left for the pub.

Opening the front door quietly, I crept in, dipping my fingers in the holy water almost without thinking and murmuring a blessing at the same time.

I moved silently, tiptoeing past the front room where Mam lay asleep on the sofa, pushing the kitchen door open, hoping it wouldn't creak. The house was in darkness. Just as I was thinking I'd missed Robert, I suddenly realised someone was standing in the room.

I gasped, suddenly fearful. The man, a black shape, took a step forwards. In the gloom of the autumn evening, now the sun had set, it was hard to see in the back room without the gas lights on.

"Where d'ye think you've been, Biddy." It was Robert's voice, more a snarl than a question.

"I...I...I've been out with Bill." There was no point lying, someone might have seen us meet at the bus stop – and anyway, I had nothing to hide, I'd done nothing wrong... or so I thought.

"What are ye doin' there Robert? You frightened me half to death." Suddenly my mouth felt dry.

Robert walked slowly toward me, each step more menacing. His face was twisted into a scowl but I could sense this was no ordinary telling-off. He seemed frightening, towering over me, and I knew that he wanted me to feel scared, even down to deliberately turning off the lighting. "Ye stay away from that Bill." Robert jabbed his finger at my chest. He kept walking until I was pinned to the wall. My whole body broke out in a sweat. I felt pure fear of this man, this brother of mine who behaved like he owned me.

Robert's face was up close to me, his eyes as cold as ice. My heart was beating, thumping in my chest so loudly it rang in my ears. Thump. Thump. Thump.

I couldn't think straight. Every sense was primed for what might be coming. My hackles were up but my defences were puny next to a working man like Robert, a man who could scythe the fields all day without breaking into sweat, who could roll a haystack and shovel wet straw with a pitchfork from dawn till dusk. No, I was hopeless against this raging force.

I stammered: "But I can't – Robert ye have to understand. I love him."

There was a moment's silence, a brief hesitation. It was the worst thing I could have said.

My voice trailed off into the soupy air, thick with my brother's pent-up fury.

Then, he lurched forward, grabbing a clump of my hair and yanking it upwards, forcing my gaze up to his.

Robert brought his face up to mine, our noses touching, the stench of his beer-soaked breath making me want to gag.

"If ye don't stay away from him, I'll make ye," he said, with deliberate slowness.

Then he pushed me violently, expelling me from his grip as easily as swatting a fly. I stumbled, grabbing at a chair for support but missing and tumbling to the floor. Just then, there was a groaning noise from the lounge, breaking the evil spell. "Ye'd better go and deal with her," said Robert, flexing his hand. He must have hurt it in shoving me. He stalked off, slamming the front door behind him. As he went he whistled his tuneless song, the sound of it making my stomach clench further.

I looked down at myself. My mouth tasted metallic, the taste of blood. I staggered up, smoothing down my skirt and testing myself to see if that was all that hurt. I looked in the cracked mirror on the mantelpiece. I'd bitten my tongue in fright.

My face looked pale next to the livid red colour. Reaching for a rag, I wiped my mouth clean, not wanting Mam to see me in such a state.

"I'm comin' Mam," I shouted, my voice still shaky, but more composed than I felt.

I took one last look at myself, then hurried into the lounge.

"Now, what's ailing ye Mam?" I said softly.

I busied around my mother, trying my best to sound cheery. I knew I couldn't burden Mam with any of this. I didn't want her to worry about Robert's controlling behaviour. What could my mother do anyway? Mam's cough racked her body day and night. She was almost permanently sodden with sherry, muttering to herself in her own little world. She couldn't walk these days and relied on me to do everything for her. To me, she looked like she was fading fast, not much longer for this world. Surprisingly the thought didn't upset me at the time. Part of me thought that perhaps Mam would finally be at peace in Jesus's arms when the day came, though I didn't let myself think about that too much, as I'd be left here alone, with Robert.

Once Mam was settled against the sofa cushions and I'd wiped her mouth and refilled her glass with alcohol, I looked around the room, grey in the twilight. The coal scuttle was empty, the fire unlit. Robert hadn't even tended to his mother while I was out. Strangely it was that thought that made me suddenly furious. If I couldn't be angry for myself, I could feel upset for our mother. I saw, as if for the first time, the shabby threadbare sofa covered by the lumpen form of our sick parent, and not for the first time, thought, *Is this what my life will be? A carer for my sick mother, a woman with no life of her own outside these walls? What will become of me?*

Just then, Mam opened her eyes. They were startlingly clear for once.

"Ok, Mam?" I asked.

"Don't ye go upsettin' Robert, he's a bad one, Biddy, a bad one..." To my memory that was the first time my mother had ever used my nickname. She'd always insisted on calling me Bridget, while my brothers and friends at school had insisted on Biddy. I felt a lump in my throat. It felt... intimate.

"Keep away from Robert, keep away from him,' she warned, before her eyes closed again, and in a few short moments she started to snore.

I stepped back, wondering if that moment's clarity had been real, as it was so unlike Mam to be aware of anything going on around her. I watched as she slept, knowing that she'd put her rare moment of lucidity to good use and in her own way had been trying to protect me. I shivered. The room was cold, so I pulled an extra blanket over Mam, kissed her on her forehead, pushing back her straggly hair and feeling a kind of sadness that things were as they were. Would I ever escape my destiny?

CHAPTER 7

GOODBYE MAMMY
November 19-28 1949

"In the name of our Lord Jesus Christ I will begin this day. I thank ye, Lord, for having preserved me during the night. I will do my best to make all I do today pleasing to You and in accordance with Your will. My dear mother Mary, watch over me this day. My Guardian Angel, take care of me. St. Joseph and all you saints of God, pray for me. Amen."

As I finished my morning prayer in front of the image of Christ's Sacred Heart above the tiled fireplace in the lounge, I crossed myself, my eyes still cast up as witness to His endless suffering. For a moment, I studied the image of Our Saviour, his heart exposed, surrounded by light yet bleeding from the thorns that circled it. Visceral and wounded, the depiction was to remind us of Jesus's death on the cross, his crown of thorns, his life given for our sins.

I prayed in the lounge every morning now so that Mam would experience my devotions as her own, giving her the little consolation she could receive from the ritual of each morning's blessing, as it gave me scant comfort. I could see every day that Mam's breathing was more laboured, her skin more grey and her will to live sliding away from us.

I prayed a lot in those days, begging for the saints to intercede for us, to help Mam stop her boozing and give her the strength to rise up from her makeshift bed, but each day her condition visibly worsened.

I stepped back, giving myself a precious silent minute to rejoin the day, the practical world around me, after those brief seconds in the spiritual realm. It was then I realised Mam's breaths were even more rasping than usual, each one sounding like a tremendous effort.

"Mam, now what's with ye this morning? Oh dear, is that breathing of yours gettin' worse?" I smiled at my mother as I crouched down next to her. She looked as if she was still sleeping.

"There, there Mammy, Biddy's here, your girl is here," I soothed, noting that her skin looked waxy, her breathing becoming more irregular.

"Ach come on ye lazy thing. It's morning and I've got some porridge on the range and a nice hot cup of tea to wake ye – Mam?"

The rasping sound had stopped. There was silence again, except for the sounds of Saturday bustle in the street, children playing hopscotch, women shooing them away so they could scrub their front steps.

I shook my mother's arm a little to try and revive her as she seemed awfully still, a waxwork dummy like the ones I'd seen at the fair a year earlier. She didn't move, didn't say a word.

"Mam? Come on now, it's me, Biddy, I've come to help ye to the lavvy then we'll have a nice cup of – oh…" Mam's skin felt odd, clammy. I touched her cheek again then pulled my hand back, recoiling as I realised the terrible truth: she had gone from me.

"Mam, Mam, come on now, wake up, d'ye hear me, wake up Mammy, please…"

My breaths came in sobs now. The truth was sinking in. I shook her, pleading for her to wake up, all the while knowing she was beyond earthly pain. I put my arms around her, holding her to me, her head flopping forward onto my chest. She had left us at last, and I was here, all alone, without a single person in the world to love me, except Bill.

"Mammy!" I cried, and broke down into sobs like a small child. I wept and railed against the terrible reality, my mother had died in my arms without the local priest to give her the last rites. I had failed her. She had passed away without the prayers that would wipe clean her sins, relieve her suffering and prepare her mortal soul for death. My only consolation was that she had been alive while I performed the morning prayer. That at least meant she had died protected by a sacred blessing, the last words she will ever have heard being a prayer. In the days that came I held onto that. It consoled me.

In the immediate minutes following her death, I amazed myself with my serenity.

I went straight round to Mrs Conroy's. My 11-year-old sister Philomena was there but, following my whispered discussion with the matriarch, she ordered Philomena to stay where she was. My sister shrugged, looked at me, her eyes questioning but I shook my head and averted my gaze. I didn't want her alarmed, so there was little fuss. We acted calmly, gathering up Mam's things, sending a local lad to tell the priest who would inform the Gardai. The father of our parish said prayers over Mam's body before the undertakers arrived. It was decided that she should be laid to rest at the Conroys' house rather than have me burdened with the responsibility of cooking, cleaning and playing host to the crowds of sympathisers who had already begun to arrive at our door bearing gifts of sandwiches and teapots for the guests. I was grateful for Philomena's grand-mother, how she took charge and left me to deal with the reality of losing my mother.

It was all very civilised, very quiet. A hush descended on the house, which even Robert didn't break when he arrived back having been told by someone that Mam had died. We watched as Mam was laid in a coffin with a shroud wrapped across her body, her face serene in the glow of the gaslight. We stared as she was lifted up and taken across our threshold for the wake a few doors down, with Robert and I trailing behind.

As it had been decreed that the wake house would be Mrs Conroy's, people from the town began to appear on her doorstep, the men holding their caps in their hands, the women bustling through to the kitchen with plates of cakes that seemed to have been produced from nowhere.

The Conroys' place looked almost exactly like ours, a tin bath hanging on a nail in the yard, an old blackened range heating the sparse kitchen that was usually strung with clothes-lines to dry reams of shirts, pants and trousers. Today the washing had been hastily piled away somewhere out of sight. The house was spotless, and goodness only knew how.

Mrs Conroy had managed to cobble together the feast that lay on the scrubbed table alongside the offerings by neighbours and friends. Piles of sandwiches, thick with butter and slices of ham, or filled with jam for the kiddies, sat on the plates. Bottles of beer and endless cups of tea were drunk.

Irish wakes were robust affairs, washed down with much beer and brandy though always with the respect due to the recently deceased.

Mam's was not like that. People trickled in, said their respects and left after a short stay, or as long as a small glass of brandy could be sipped and a sandwich nibbled. Mam had become a shadow figure in the village. Everyone knew her propensity for drink and her increasing infirmity as a result, and they kept their distance. It was how it was, and I didn't think them particularly cruel or callous.

I left as soon as I could, though the wake would go on through the night and into the next day, as a vigil was kept for the newly departed soul. Even though it was my mother's wake, I felt like an outsider in Mrs Conroy's home. Shutting my front door behind me, I leaned against it for a moment before performing the ritual ablution with Holy water.

Just then, I heard a scuffle from the kitchen, and raised male voices. *What in Our Lady's name is going on?* I thought, moving cautiously into the back room.

Robert was glaring at Jimmie, who looked equally fierce. They stood opposite each other, the table between them, like two bulls meaning to charge.

"What's happening? Why are ye two fightin' today of all days? The day our mammy died!" I said, in shocked tones.

"Keep out of this, Bridget," sneered Robert.

Jimmie glanced at me, his face red, looking fit to burst.

"No, stay, Biddy. Ye can hear what your scum brother has tried to do. He's tried to steal Mam's inheritance from ye. Though with all his cleverness, he's just found out there's nothing to steal!" Jimmie laughed mirthlessly.

"Our father had land, I found the papers," said Robert. "It's mine by rights now that Mam is dead. Michael is out of the picture and so there's just me. I'm the one who stayed here and supported her."

At that Jimmie laughed again. His face looked dangerous in the darkening room.

"You've never given a thought about anyone else in your life since the day ye were born, Robert. Mam knew that. I know that. Biddy knows it."

I coughed with fright, not wanting to be a pawn in this game of words. Words I didn't completely understand.

"There was land. Yes I did search through Mam's stuff, so what? Just because I thought of looking for this before ye, that's what you're sore about," shouted Robert, brandishing a piece of aged paper in front of Jimmie's face, like a red rag to an already raging bull.

"It means nothing, there is nothing," countered Jimmie. "Jaysus Christ you're so goddamned stupid!"

Robert looked as if he would launch at his brother but I cut in before he could act.

"What d'ye mean Robert? Mam had no money! Look at the way we live – no-one can be daft enough to think there's a pot of gold in this house!" I snorted.

Robert swivelled his head, his eyes boring into me. "The. Way. We. Live?" He took time saying each word individually.

Feeling alarmed, I stepped back, but Robert saw my weakness.

"I put food on the table. I go out and work at dawn every day God gives me, and ye complain about the livin' standards like some high-and-mighty rich girl. I'll show ye what your ingratitude gets ye…"

Robert raised his fist but I screamed: "I won't be here Robert. I'm leavin' to marry Bill. He's asked me and I said yes. D'ye hear me, I said 'Yes'. I don't care about some land or money. I don't care about any of that, I just want to get away from you." I knew I would regret saying it, but I was past all reason or sense by that point.

Robert's voice became suddenly calm and steady, which was somehow more frightening than his anger.

"I'm head of the house now, and I say to ye Biddy that you're not marryin' that no-good Bill. You're a whore for runnin' round with him, a WHORE. I'm in charge and what I say goes from now on, so ye'd better tell that bastard that he won't get his hands on ye. You're soiled goods and you're not goin' anywhere."

Robert drew himself up to his full height, his eyes glinting, nasty. Jimmie reacted quickly. He raced round to stand in front of me and said in a voice as cold as Robert's heart: "Ye won't tell Biddy, or anybody else what to do. You've bullied her enough over the years, leave her and Bill in peace."

For a moment nothing happened, and I started to think that Robert would back down, walk away. How wrong I was. I also realised that it was probably Jimmie who had sanctioned Bill and I courting, and it was probably him that had stopped Robert breaking us up.

In a flash, Robert launched himself at Jimmie, punching him, grabbing his suit, his one smart shirt. Fabric ripped. A chair was thrown. I ducked down, cowering in the corner of the room, unable to look at the carnage.

"STOP, just STOP IT!" I screamed but they didn't hear me, or they didn't want to hear me. That second, the table was overturned with a shout of "Ye bastard!" then a kick, more scuffling and a groan of pain.

"You've been wantin' to do this for years," goaded Jimmie, which was greeted by a sickening moan as fist impacted bone. The pair rolled on the floor, plates crashing off the mantelpiece, furniture kicked out of their way.

Jimmie scrabbled up. He took a long look at me while Robert caught his breath, as if to say…what? I will never know. In the next moment he was gone, dashing out of the house with Robert in hot pursuit. I lay there as darkness fell, trembling and finally letting the tears of the day fall.

Jimmie was the only family I had left now. The only one who could defend me against Robert and his fury. As the evening wore on I waited for Jimmie to return, to tell me it was all ok, that Robert would never hurt me, or call me names, or watch me with that intense longing, ever again, but he didn't come.

Hours later, Robert returned, his lip cut and bleeding, his fists sliced and his clothes hanging off him. He wouldn't say what had happened. All he said was that I was never to mention Jimmie's name, or Bill's, in the house again. Confused and frightened, I slept on Mam's sofa that night, a light, tense sleep, like an animal on the alert for danger. The next morning Robert left the house at daybreak, the door slamming after him, and I waited and waited for Jimmie to come and find me.

I didn't know it but that was the last time I would ever see my brother Jimmie. Perhaps he ran away, though that was hard to believe as he would never have left me completely. Perhaps there was a more sinister explanation? The brothers had fought since they were born, and it always felt it would end up with a fight to the death, and perhaps that's what happened? I never knew. I never heard from Jimmie again. It was as if, from that moment, he didn't exist. My feelings of desolation and abandonment were complete.

I dragged my aching bones through that next day, praying for my Jimmie, praying that I would some day see him again, though a cold chill of fear had settled at the base of my spine, a kind of 'knowing' that I would search for him in vain. I had no family left. No-one. With a heavy heart, I went back to Mrs Conroy's to sit with those who'd stayed overnight, to pour tea, to listen to whispered words of sympathy, to flay my heart open for the mother, brother and sister I had lost. Grief swelled within me, taking root inside my hollow shell of a body. I felt anchorless, adrift, yet somehow free. I had made a decision. I had nothing left to stay here for. My losses piled on top of each other and they served to show me that all I had now in the world was Bill, my saviour, my sweetheart. How I loved him. He had asked me to marry him, and despite Robert's insistence never to mention his name again, I vowed to myself to fly out of the nest that was choking me, into a life that would truly be my own. I said nothing of this to Robert, or to any of the people who attended Mam's wake. I hugged my secret to myself. I really was going to leave Templemore for good, and sadly, the thought brought me nothing but comfort.

I never asked Robert about any land or inheritance, and I can only imagine it was more wishful thinking on Robert's part, but again, I never got to the bottom of it, and I didn't care to either. Money, and the pursuit of it, has never been important to me, and it wasn't then. It was love that mattered, my love for Bill, and my hopes and dreams for our future.

I walked slowly back to my empty home and looked around. Robert was sluicing his wounds in the scullery.

Mam's faded apron hung by the mantelpiece, next to a pile of dirty dishes, the chairs and table littered the room. Slowly, as if recovering from a long illness, I stood up, put the room back together, taking off my coat and replacing it with the apron I had been destined to wear since I was a child.

I didn't cry after that initial shock of my mother's death. I felt that over the years I'd shed enough tears for her, for our damaged family, for Patrick and then because of Robert. My tears had all been used up. I was now an orphan, entirely reliant on the brother who frightened and bullied me. And so a new emotion crept in over the following days – trepidation.

I felt like I was in a bubble, somehow separate from the events of the wake in the days leading to the funeral. I would nod my head, thank those who came to Mrs Conroy's door, receive their offerings of food and candles, then shut the door, thankful for the return to peace, though it was the calm before the storm and I didn't know it.

I crept around Robert, doing whatever he asked of me, getting dinner on the table at exactly the moment he walked in, washing his shirts, laying them out to dry in front of the range each evening, whilst praying and praying for Mam's soul.

"Bless me Father for I have sinned." I whispered.

The wooden grille in the confessional box separating me from the priest cast a patterned orange glow against his features.

"It has been two weeks since my last confession and here are my sins. I have despaired of God's mercy when my mammy died. I have taken too much drink. I stole from my Mam's sherry jug, taking a cup each evening to help me sleep. I have not been chaste in thoughts about my sweetheart Bill. I have let him touch me in sinful places though I am still a virgin. I have wished ill on my brother for his treatment of me, and I am sorry for all these, and the sins of my past life."

The priest started to intone the prayers for my penance, but instead I cut him off.

I had come to confession for the first time since Mam died, a week earlier. All week something had been troubling me, something stuck in the back of my mind that now had to come out or I felt I would scream. I knew my mother was a sinner, taking too much alcohol, living with Patrick without a wedding, though I never knew this for sure, and she died without the priest's last rites being performed. I was convinced that because of all this my mam's soul was now stuck in the fires of Purgatory, the final painful purification before entering Heaven. This knowledge was keeping me awake at nights, and meant I reached more and more for the comforts of the sherry jug, hence putting my own soul in mortal danger. I had to do something. I had to relieve my mother's state somehow.

"Please let me have Mam's sins. Father, let me go to Purgatory or Hell instead of her when I die. I have sinned greatly, and so if ye give me hers, too, it won't make much difference. I reckon I'm bound for Hell anyway."

Inside, I felt this to be true. Even though I'd looked after my family, cared for Mam, helped bring up my adored sister, I felt somehow outside of God's Grace. It was a feeling that had grown in me since a child, from the first seeds of revolt against the nuns who taught us our scriptures, to the envy I felt for my brothers and their carefree way of life. Or perhaps it was donning Mam's apron each day, saying a blessing to Our Lady and wondering why it was me that was bound to the church's strictures, and not my brothers. Then when I felt desire for the first time with Bill, and saw the desire I impelled in another, my brother Robert, perhaps that was when I felt my soul starting to slide away like jelly slipping from its mould. Or perhaps it was all the loss I had suffered making me feel like I somehow didn't deserve God's love, His church or the love of my religious community? Who can say.

I felt I would always be a sinner so what use was confession or penance anyway? No use to me. In my grief-adled mind, this made perfect sense, and so I thought I should layer Mam's sins onto mine as I was surely living, and would die, outside of God's Grace anyway.

The priest shifted in his seat.

The thought hit me. Perhaps I had too many sins to take on Mam's? That idea made my insides freeze.

"But I'm also a good girl. I looked after Mam. I look after my brother Robert. I love my sister Philomena. Please Father, please let me have Mam's sins, I can't bear to think of her trapped in Purgatory. Sometimes at night I think I can hear her screams…"

At this, the priest cleared his throat.

"Child, ye must pray for your mother's soul, to reduce her punishment. Offer up Holy Communion, attend Mass more frequently, not just each Sunday but daily, and offer partial Indulgences. These are things ye can do, but ye cannot take on her sins, no, ye cannot do that…God bless you." He gave me my penance in the form of Hail Mary's.

"Thank you Father." I crossed myself and left the dark confines of the confessional. I walked quickly from the church, my shoes tapping the stone floor, desperate to get outside, to breathe in the Godless air and fill my lungs. I could not save Mam from further pain. I could not influence the Almighty's decision, who even now had placed Mam even further out of reach from me. My heart was filled with sorrow. I walked and walked that day, not wanting to go home, the sight of the familiar things, the places she sat, her slippers waiting for her feet, even the cup by the sofa that had contained her sherry; these things were too much, too raw, too much a reminder of my utter helplessness.

Eight days before Mam died it was my 21st birthday, my coming-of-age. Yet the day had been spent performing my usual duties, housebound except for a quick dash to the shops to buy in bread and vegetables for the dinner. That evening had passed quietly. I sat with Mam, Robert was out at the pub as it was a Friday night, and so I chatted to her, giving her a snippet of the local gossip, who was 'in trouble' by whom and when they'd marry, how Mrs Flanigan had a poorly knee, how so-and-so's son had left school to work in Dublin. Our lives were small. There had been great events in Southern Ireland – or the Republic of Ireland – as we were now called after obtaining independence from the British Commonwealth earlier in the year (18th April 1949), but the ripples of this had barely trickled down except to provide more for neighbours to talk about over their yard fences. It seemed a monumental step to me. I liked the idea of independence, but perhaps that was because I yearned for it so much myself. I remember nothing but sadness from that night of my birthday with Mam. She nodded and blinked as I spoke, sometimes leaning forwards to cough then falling back, exhausted and pale. I kept up the stream of chat, as much to keep my anxiety about her at bay as to calm her. She had been prone to fits of anger, though could do little about it, hunched on the sofa, a blanket over her knees looking for all her 51 years like an old woman.

I could barely believe that just over two weeks earlier I'd had the birthday that made me officially a woman, and I was determined now to tell Robert that I would marry Bill, and leave Templemore. I was free at last.

We stood shivering in the winter cold, black figures like crows against the ground, bleached white with early frost. We listened to the funeral service performed by the priest, his words ebbing and flowing through the ceremony. It was my brother Michael who scattered the first clods of earth onto her coffin, which had been the cheapest that the undertaker could provide.

I turned away, not wanting to remember Mam as she had

been in her final years, wanting instead to recall the woman who had joked and been happy enough with me as a child, who had shooed me away from the range while she cooked stew and sat each evening by the fire, catching up on her sewing or knitting. The woman I sat with each day as a young woman was so different. The drink had ravaged her, but it was her heart that finally gave out, too much sadness, perhaps, from the death of her first husband. I don't reckon she ever got over that, not really. Left to bring up her children, one a newborn, by herself. Her life had been tough, and even now I couldn't save her from the pain of Purgatory, the interim of suffering that would finally cleanse her of sin and let her enter Heaven. But when would that be? No-one, not the priest, not Mrs Conroy or any of the neighbouring women I'd asked, had an answer. She suffered in death as in life, and I couldn't bear it.

The bright spot at the funeral was my brother Michael, now 30, being there with his wife Mary and their two small children, Eric and Angela, from Dublin. I had greeted them with genuine joy. I missed Michael's steady influence and his position as eldest son, meaning that Robert's behaviour was kept in check while he was around. I was becoming increasingly uncomfortable sharing the house with Robert. He watched me all the time, yet barely grunted at me. The house simmered with tension, and I didn't know how or when it was going to explode.

Jimmie was noticeably absent at the graveside, and I dared not ask Robert where he was. Michael asked after him and there were mutterings from others about him not being there but I shut my ears to it. Robert told them that Jimmie had taken off after Mammy died and he had no idea where he'd gone. But somehow I knew that Jimmie was gone for good, I knew it in my bones. I kept my grief separate from that for my mother, as I feared being overwhelmed. There would be time aplenty in future to unpick those wounds, bring each one to the light for healing, and the time wasn't now. Anyway, I was going to marry my beloved and leave this place, and my memories, behind. My mind was made up.

Robert, his face set hard, oversaw the funeral. Michael left immediately after the ceremony, saying it was a long trip back to the city. I waved them off but neither Michael nor his family looked back. The atmosphere at Mam's grave had been subdued. To my memory, no-one except Philomena cried. At the time I couldn't even comfort her as she clung to her grandmother, Mrs Conroy, which broke my heart afresh. Once upon a time it would have been me she would have clung to for comfort or reassurance but that time had passed. I hadn't talked to my sister much since Mam died, caught up as I was in my own grief but also uncertain about what I could say to make it all better. It must have been a confusing and unsettling time for my poor sister. Her mum had died, a mum she barely knew, but her mum all the same. I didn't know how she would begin to understand that. But she had her grandparents, Mrs Conroy wrapping her in love and protecting her like a lioness.

Sad though I was about the space between us now, I was also glad that she had been removed from the unhappiness surrounding Mam. She was better off where she was and I knew she was happy there, so I did not fear leaving her behind when I started my new life with Bill.

It was time for me to move on from all the loss and sadness. But, unbeknown to me, my future, the one I had started to imagine could become real, had been quashed before it had begun. My brother Robert had gone to Bill's that terrible evening of the fight with Jimmie, perhaps on a pal's tractor or horse and cart, and had threatened him with some horror, forcing him to leave Ireland. Robert's reputation as a hard man, a violent man, was evidently not limited to Templemore, as that night, the night I lost my mother and brother, I also lost the love of my life, Bill.

After the last of the mourners had left, I walked beside Robert back to the house, willing myself to have faith and courage enough to say what had to be said.

"Robert, I want ye to know that I'm leavin' tonight. I'm goin' to Bill's village and I won't be comin' back. There's no point stopping me or followin' me as he'll stop ye, so he will. He loves me, and I intend to be his wife."

There was silence for a moment. I gulped, fear rising like acid in my belly.

Robert barked a short laugh.

I turned, momentarily surprised. That wasn't the reaction I'd expected.

He looked at me, clearly delighting in my confusion.

"Ye really don't know do ye?" he snarled.

I shook my head, afraid to say something wrong. What was happening? Why wasn't he yelling at me that I was a 'disgrace' or a 'whore'?

"He's gone, I made sure of it," he said, watching my face intently for the moment when I realised my dreams had turned to dust.

"What do ye mean, gone?" I managed to keep my voice steady though my heart was pounding.

"Ye don't think I was goin' to let ye leave with that eejet, do ye? No, Biddy, that was never goin' to happen. I went there, spoke to him myself, told him if he didn't leave Ireland on the first boat to England then I'd kill him with my bare hands."

Was this some kind of sick joke?

Again, my instincts told me it wasn't.

"Ye didn't hurt him?" I eventually whispered, forcing myself to hold Robert's gaze.

"No, I didn't hurt your precious loverboy, not much anyway, but he left, oh yes Biddy, he left without a goodbye. He didn't stay. He didn't tell me he'd kill me first. He's a coward and he left that night, and ye'll never see him again as long as you live."

Robert stalked off, leaving me standing in the graveyard, shivering with cold, wishing the hard ground would open and swallow me up. In my heart I knew that Bill had gone. He hadn't come to the funeral. I hadn't heard from him at all since Mam died, and I'd told myself he didn't want to make a scene with Robert, that he was better off not coming, but the painful truth was that he had left me, abandoned me like all the others. I stood there, as bereft and desolate as I've ever felt, wondering how on earth I would go on living now that everyone I'd ever loved was lost to me.

CHAPTER 8
ALONE AND FRIGHTENED
Spring 1950

All of my dreams and hopes of happiness were buried that day along with my mother. But while something inside me had died and my sorrows were all-encompassing, life carried on in its own way. I walked down to the main street in Templemore most days, carrying my basket and list of provisions, avoiding the local women when I could, exchanging pleasantries only when I had to.

In the general store, with its horsehair brooms stacked upright against the shop window, Mrs Murphy nattered away in my ear as I searched among the scrubbing brushes, soap and candles for the cheapest carbolic soap. I nodded politely to her, unable to raise even the barest of smiles.

"It doesn't seem right that a young girl like yourself should waste her life away cleanin' for that brother of yours," declared Mrs Murphy.

I knew she meant no harm by it, but her words changed nothing in my life and so I barely heard them.

"You're a fine-lookin' girl, Biddy, ye'd have all the boys queuing up to court ye if you only got out a bit more. It's good to go to Mass every day, but ye'll never meet anyone unless ye go to a farm dance like the other girls."

A stout, talkative woman, Mrs Murphy liked putting her nose in other people's business, but she had a good heart and I couldn't dislike her – especially as she was absolutely right in her advice.

Every month the church helped the farmers find their wives by putting on a dance. They were really the only chance young people got to socialise and meet romantic partners, but I had avoided them. I didn't want one of the other boys, or men, as they were now. I wanted my Bill, and next to him the others all paled into insignificance, with their red hair and stilted conversation. I wanted my bold, confident, charming sweetheart.

But he had fled, leaving me behind, without anyone to protect me or care for me. I loved him but I hated him as well. I hated him for leaving me, for not standing up to Robert, for fleeing from me like a hound with his tail between his legs. And yet, even as I felt this, I knew no-one could stand up to Robert. He was a menace, and a man to be feared. Despite this, I wished Bill had come for me and whisked me away to England, too, where we could've been free to be together. I still hadn't heard from Jimmie. It seemed that the two men, the two last remaining points of happiness in my life, had both disappeared like the incense trailing from the altar server's thurible at Mass. Gone, as if made of vapour.

I sighed heavily. My mind was still reeling from the shock of Bill leaving, and mixed in with the pain of my sweetheart's desertion were Jimmie's sudden disappearance and Mammy's death. I was so shellshocked that I barely knew how to put one foot in front of the other. I couldn't make sense of my life at all.

"Come on dearie, don't ye be sad about how things turned out. Ye'll find a man to court ye before long." And with that well-meaning but insensitive comment, Mrs Murphy bustled off to speak to a friend. She'd mistaken my sigh for one of yearning for a boyfriend, and nothing could have been further from the truth. If I couldn't have Bill, I didn't want anyone.

"Two bars of carbolic and a large box of matches please," I said, taking coins from my purse and placing them on the counter. I put the wrapped package into my basket and turned to go back home where the week's washing was waiting for me.

The thought of the weekly wash made my heart sink – it was backbreaking, painful and time-consuming work but it had to be done. Once indoors, I pulled on the apron, and took out one of the bars of soap. It had to be grated by hand into the endless kettles of boiling water I would pour into our tin bath, which also doubled as the wash basin. My hands were now permanently chapped and sore, especially after winter, when the cold increased the abrasion of my skin. Using a big copper stick, I'd then lift out the shirts, pants, trousers and skirts after first using the water for the sheets, and would then rinse them in the scullery with cold water. I'd drag the wet clothes through the mangle, sweating as I turned the handle grindingly slowly. Each time I passed them through I had to rinse again with cold water to get the last of the soap out.

A wash would take all day before I could finally hang the sheets over the clothes line that stretched across the yard, and drape the clothes over chairs next to the range to dry. Whenever it rained, I had to throw sheets over the lines that hung in the kitchen, the back room becoming more like a washhouse, and smelling of steam and carbolic. I lathered Vaseline on my hands all winter to help with the 'chaps' as we called it, but come the springtime they were still sore-looking, not that I cared. Looking back, it is obvious to me that I was lost in heavy grief that winter spanning 1949 and the beginning of 1950: I mourned not only the loss of my family members, but also Bill, whose name I never even whispered, except to ask myself *Why didn't ye take me with ye?*

At first I couldn't believe that Bill would have, could have, left me. After Robert told me he'd given Bill his marching orders, I still waited for him on the very next visit he was due to see me.

Just as I'd done all those months previously, I stood at the bus stop as people piled off the bus and looked for those who were meeting them. Every time I used to see Bill's mop of blond hair my heart leapt in my chest and I ran forward, not caring how eager I looked. I was a young woman, passionately in love, and I wanted Bill to know how he had stolen my heart. I had nothing to hide. I told him time and time again, he owned all of me, and I him, and we kissed when I said that, and planned our wedding over and over again.

But that day Bill didn't get off the bus. His beautiful blond head was absent, his lightness of step, his grace and confidence, all were gone. He had left me, had left Ireland for good. I only really understood it in those seconds, when the bus emptied then re-filled with new passengers, and I stood by the roadside staring as people pushed by. The locals all knew by now that Robert had warned Bill off me, it was no secret, and I was sure I heard a few whispers from clumps of women by the bus stop that day, but I didn't care about that either. I was in shock, finally realising that Robert had spoken the truth to me when he'd said: "I told your *boyfriend* he wasn't welcome here, and if he ever set foot on Irish soil again he was a dead man." Robert had emphasised the word boyfriend in a sneering kind of way as if it was an obscenity. I saw no sin in love, no harm in passion, only that Robert would never know it, or worse, never receive it from anyone, and that made me feel pity for him. That pity helped me through the following months as winter set in, the temperature plummeted and I thought I'd never feel warm again, as we lived together in an uneasy truce.

Once the light started creeping back, snowdrops pushed through the frost and spring began to re-emerge, I realised how bleak my life had become, and yet how little I cared about any of it. My heart had been ripped from me. It felt like my soul had been taken as well.

Of course, I hated living with Robert. I crept around him, scared of saying or doing anything that displeased him. He was the man of the house and I his servant, yet there was more. I knew his eyes continued to follow me and it made me shiver more than the cold ever could. Robert's drinking had also increased, and in a strange way I was grateful for it, as it meant he spent more time at the pub than at home. Most nights he'd roll in just after 11pm, attempt to spoon his stew into his mouth, then stumble up the stairs to his room. I didn't dare go to my bed till I knew he was asleep, his snores rattling through the thin floorboards, reassuring me it was safe to go upstairs at last. The weeks passed, and the tension between Robert and myself increased steadily. He didn't bother to hide his stares. He didn't turn away or make an excuse as he had when Mam was alive. If he was near me, he'd brush my arm with his hand as I put his dish of stew on the table, or he'd stand too close to me, pressing his body against mine as he passed me in the hallway. I stayed out of his way as much as I could but I had nowhere else to go, nowhere to stay, no-one to protect me. Robert was all I had, the only family in the world now, yet all I wanted was to get as far away from him as I could.

My fears were proved right.

Crash.

The front door flew open.

"Where's me feckin' key. What have ye done with it, whore." Robert's snarl startled me. I was dozing in the kitchen as the last embers of the range burned orange, emitting a gentle heat.

"Where are ye, ye feckin' whore of a sister?"

I jumped up, all my senses on full alert, my back to the wall.

Robert staggered in, kicking open the kitchen door with one hobnail boot, wiping his hand over the stubble on his chin.

Before I could say a word, he'd marched over to me and grabbed me by my hair.

"What is it, what's happened?" I whimpered.

"Don't ye speak to me, don't ye EVER feckin' speak to me. Ye don't deserve to say a word in this house, whore. They've been laughin' at ye in the pub, sayin' ye'll do for anyone now, sayin' you'll whore yourself out for anyone with a coin in his pocket."

I wriggled out of his grip, pushing him back against the wall. I must have caught him at a weak angle because he tripped back, letting go of me.

"They're lyin', it's all lies!" I yelled back at him. "Who is sayin' all this? Why would they say something so wicked?"

My mind whirled. I knew that whoever had said those terrible things about me was aiming their spite at Robert, attacking him by calling me a prostitute. The pettiness stung but I didn't have time to acknowledge it. Robert was leering, staggering toward me with a look of pure cruelty on his face. Something about the insult seemed to have broken the thin veneer of respectability we had maintained at home. I knew this instinctively. Calling me a whore had unleashed something animal in him, something of the hunter for the hunted. I bolted in panic.

I darted up the stairs and into my bedroom, curling up on my bed and placing the thin pillow over my ears to drown out his curses. It was the worst thing I could've done. I should've left that house, run for safety, but instead I caught myself in his trap.

The heavy tread of Robert's boots on the stairs told me he was coming. I started to shake, my whole body seized up in terror. What was happening?

My door opened, and Robert stood swaying in the entrance to my room, the bulk of his body dark, his face glowering.

I peeped out of my pillow. There was no sanctuary for me to run to. In my innocence and confusion, I'd thought that he wouldn't trespass into my room. I was wrong.

He stood for a moment, his eyes glinting, as if sizing up his next actions. That's how I knew that what came next wasn't a crime of passion, a swell of oceanic emotion that rendered him a slave to his anger, his building fury. No, he was coldly surveying me and the room. He was thinking. His actions were intentional, and it was this knowledge that froze me to the core.

I jumped up, somehow knowing now what was coming. Time slowed down. Robert moved towards me. I was helpless. I had nowhere to run, nowhere to hide, no-one to help me. I was alone – and terrified. The bed creaked as he pushed me back onto it. My body started convulsing with shock and yet I couldn't physically move. Even my screams stayed caught in my throat. With a slow, slow gesture, he undid his stays, dropping his trousers and thick cotton underwear to the floor. I held his gaze, refusing to look at his manliness, and that enraged him.

Grabbing my hair again, he pulled me to him, forcing his

mouth onto mine, the bitter taste of the ale he'd drunk and cigarettes he'd smoked on his tongue. I tried to cry out but I couldn't.

"Lift up your skirts," he ordered. I shook my head.

"Lift up your feckin' skirts. You're a whore, all the lads in the village say it to my face now. To my face! D'ye know how that feels, Bridget? You're no good for any man, that's what they say, that you're a whore who deserves no better."

"Please, Robert, I'm your sister, please don't do this," I begged, at last finding my voice. This was a mortal sin, a place neither of us could come back from. He was putting both our souls in peril and I had to find a way to stop him.

"Please, please, please... it's a sin Robert."

In reply he hit me, slapping across my face with the back of his hand.

"It's no sin to feck a whore, an' that's all ye are to me now." My hair was held tightly in his grip.

He pulled me to him again so our noses touched, his hard eyes staring into mine.

"They all say you're a whore so what do we do with whores, hey?"

"No, no, please Robert." I wept, but my tears only seemed to fuel his desire, excite him further. He was panting now.

"When I tell you to do something you do it, d'ye hear me ye little bitch? What did ye do for him, eh? Did ye enjoy it, whore, did ye?" Robert's fury was incandescent. He scrabbled for my skirt, tearing my knickers and forcing his flesh inside mine. His weight pinned me to the bed.

He hurled curse after curse, his spittle falling on my face as he ploughed into me, hurting me.

"Get off me ye bastard!" I shouted, trying to struggle free

but he was bigger and stronger than me.

"You'll do what I tell you to do." Robert's face was red. He was reaching his climax, his face inches from mine, I struggled furiously… then suddenly I shrank away from him.

Something changed and it was as if I disconnected from that room and the unholy act Robert was forcing me to endure. I saw myself as if from above, looking down on Robert, seeing me stiff as a board underneath him, staring back at myself.

I don't know if it was a form of self-defence or a way of coping, but I lay there as he finished as if it was somebody else experiencing it. I opened my mouth but no noise came out, I had disappeared somewhere deep inside myself.

Seconds later Robert was fumbling with his breeches and I looked over at him, almost as if I hadn't noticed what he'd done. My clothes were ripped where he had clawed at me, and I saw that I was stained with blood. My wrists were red with marks left by his fingers as he'd held me down to brutalise me. I looked at these things as if I had no connection to them whatsoever. Call it shock, or trauma, but I felt as if the old Biddy, the one who existed before, had died, leaving me in her place. Robert pushed back his oily hair, grunted something I didn't hear and left the room.

I lay there staring at the ceiling for several minutes before I suddenly burst into tears, which ran hot down my face. I got up off the bed and went to my washbasin, where with a clean rag, I attempted to wipe myself. My arms were trembling and I kept spilling the water down my legs. Gingerly I took off my skirt and proceeded to rip it into strips, which I then threw on the unlit coal fire in my room. I would burn them tomorrow, I just had to get through the night. I crept down to the kitchen and found the bottle of brandy that, in those days, was always kept in the home for medical purposes. I poured out a cupful and slowly carried it back upstairs.

Crawling back to bed, I curled up again after downing the contents of that cup, hoping for the sweet oblivion it promised. I waited all night long for dawn to break, unable to move, unable to comprehend the nightmare my life had become, tears rolling down my cheeks but without uttering even a sigh.

CHAPTER 9
BRIDGET'S SECRET
September 1950

My hands circled the round swell of my stomach, tracing the new hill of my body tenderly, feeling the insistent kick of the little feet inside me. Sitting on my bed, looking out of the window at the golden autumn light as it shimmered over the steeple of Sacred Heart Church, I also felt the tug of anxiety that grew stronger each day as my pregnancy advanced.

The child inside me was a product of rape, yet I felt nothing for it but love. Feeling the new life grow within me had somehow helped me to get through the past five months since my brother defiled me, took my virginity, in the most brutal way possible. Robert had never mentioned that evening. I didn't even know if he remembered it because of his heavy drinking, but something told me he did. He still looked at me, but was it my imagination, or did he refuse to meet my eyes? Perhaps in shame for what he'd done? Perhaps in revolt for the sin he had committed? I took his lead and hadn't said a word, hoping that by being quiet and melting into the background as much as I could, I would deflect his unnerving gaze and, so far, it seemed to have worked.

Despite the change in season, the day was still warm, yet when the time came to ease myself off the bed and get ready for Mass, I was grateful to pull on my heavy winter coat so I could wrap it around my changing form and so avert the interest and speculation of Templemore's gossips and housewives.

I knew I couldn't get away with my condition for long. Someone would spot it. I was amazed they hadn't already as I was putting on weight by the day, my features filling out, my ankles starting to swell as the pregnancy advanced.

"Come on, my darlin', let's go and say our prayers. We don't want the wrath of God upon us as well as that of Templemore, so we don't," I whispered to my baby and its feet kicked harder at the gentle sound of my voice.

'You're a feisty one today, but I know where ye get that from," I said with a sigh, as I pulled the scratchy wool layer over me. It was far too warm to wear it, but I had no choice. I didn't know what would happen to the baby or me once everyone knew. I wasn't able to think any more than a day or two ahead of myself. I couldn't.

The enormity of my situation, the fragility of it, was so overwhelming that I simply couldn't put my mind to it. I think I was still in shock. I was carrying my brother's child, through an act condemned by God. In my heart I knew I was outside of His jurisdiction now, with only my word against Robert's that the attack took place at all. I had no-one to turn to. Mrs Conroy and her family had turned their backs on me after Mam died. The shame of Mam's drinking hadn't been forgotten, or so it seemed to me, though I never really knew why they excluded me from Philomena's life and theirs after Mam's death. I can only assume they wanted a clean break with our family. They weren't unkind to me. No words were said, but I felt their coldness, the lack of welcome at their door and I cringed away, feeling somehow marked by our family's disgrace.

Philomena had now been unofficially adopted by Daniel Conroy, Patrick's elder brother, and his wife Mary, and they had moved out of Templemore. I begged Mrs Conroy to tell me where they'd taken her but she always shook her head sadly, as if the knowledge was a burden to her. I begged her. I even shouted once. I knocked and knocked at their front door, but no-one came, no-one would tell me where she was and why they'd felt they had to take her away.

I never saw her again – and my grief at the loss of her piled on top of the loss of everyone else I'd loved. Jimmie had disappeared completely after that fight with Robert. In my whole life I never heard from him again. I never knew what happened to him and I never dared ask Robert. So I was left to mourn him as well, not knowing if he was still in Ireland, or even if he was alive or dead, though my instinct told me that if he was alive he would've found me, come back to see me, and he never did.

There was nobody I could turn to, and the thought of going to confession to tell the priest what had happened chilled me to the bone. I'd drawn on my faith for strength in the past, but this time was different. I felt disconnected from God, from the Catholic faith, as if I'd already been expelled for the wickedness that had been enacted on me.

"Ach, my back's hurtin' littl' one," I crooned as I rubbed my lower back. In a funny way, I felt I only had my baby to talk to now. "If we don't hurry, we'll be late for Mass and ye know how Father Connor hates latecomers. We'll go for a walk afterwards and soak up some of that sunshine."

Walking to the church, I stopped for a moment and held my face up to the sun.

"Biddy, ye'll boil to death in that coat, now why don't ye run home and leave it there, you've got time." One of the local women had stopped to admonish me for my choice of clothing.

"I'm feeling a bit under the weather, so it'll be fine, Mrs O'Grady, don't ye worry about me," I replied, making sure my voice was upbeat to swerve any questions. I had to keep my bump hidden at all costs and I couldn't have nosy old ladies ordering me back home!

"Ach go on with ye. Mind ye don't faint in this heat, it's more like summer than autumn," added the nodding, white-haired matron before she walked off up the long pathway to the church entrance. I could see the priest at the doorway, wearing his flowing vestment and shaking the hands of everyone as they entered.

I made sure to keep walking, keeping my eyes down. People tended to avoid me nowadays and I didn't mind. I didn't want their feigned concern, their pity, after Mam's death. I wanted to be left alone, locked in my own emotions, separate from the community I'd grown up within.

Everyone in Templemore, unless they were ill or dying, would come to Mass on Sunday. It was unthinkable to skip the service. Most would have been to confession on Saturday evening in order to wipe their sins and start afresh, except for me. I couldn't go. I wouldn't go. Deep down, I knew that what I had to confess would break my life apart, and I wasn't ready, not yet. Despite my reluctance to attend, I still sought spiritual peace, a gentle guide to point me in the direction of my future – our future – me and my unborn child. I hoped and prayed there was some way we could stay together, but heaven only knew how that would happen. Unmarried girls who got themselves into trouble were condemned as sinners, and rushed off to mysterious mother-and-baby homes where they'd return months later with flat bellies and no sign of the child they'd given birth to. I shivered when I thought of those young women, refusing to align my fate with theirs though knowing I had few other options, if any. The identity of my baby's father deepened my fears. I wanted to stay in a state of denial, in my own little bubble where I talked to my baby, rubbed my growing tummy and hoped for a future that he or she belonged in, too.

I slipped into a pew at the back of the church as the first stirrings of the organ began, crossing myself automatically as I entered the sacred building. Too late, I realised I'd sat next to one of my neighbours, a pinch-faced woman with sharp eyes and a sharper tongue. I generally avoided her.

Mrs O'Sullivan looked me up and down pointedly, and I pulled my coat round me protectively. I could feel prickles of sweat across my back and under my arms, which made me even more uncomfortable.

"Ye can't be cold, so you can't. Why're ye wearing that old coat of yours, eh Biddy?" she asked sharply. The priest's voice began intoning the start of the service. The pews were packed, the air felt suddenly hot and the altar, which I could barely see, began swimming in front of my eyes, the light becoming like jewels against the back of my eyelids.

Oh Jaysus, I'm goin' to faint... I thought to myself. Don't faint, don't ye dare…. I dug my nails into my palms to try and stop it, but the woozy feeling only increased and I crumpled into a swoon. The light went yellow then black, then I felt myself being moved, voices murmuring around me, the feel of a hard seat under me. I blinked and shook my head.

"Here ye go, Biddy, drink this water, it'll help you," came Mrs O'Sullivan's voice and a glass was placed in my hand.

"Thank you," I stammered, feeling for my coat. To my horror

I realised it wasn't there. I was sitting in a side room, two local women bustling around me, in my normal dress, which revealed the growing mound of my belly.

"Drink it, it'll help the littl' one," came a kindly voice. A younger woman with strawberry-red hair, who I only knew vaguely from trips into town, smiled at me and tipped the glass gently to my mouth.

"You fell over as ye tried to get up and knocked your head on the pew. Are ye both ok?" said the woman, not quite meeting my eyes.

So my pregnancy was obvious then. I looked down to see it protruding from my dress and I felt shamed into silence.

"So, you've a secret, Biddy Larkin? Well, ye won't be the first girl to get yourself in this condition, and ye won't be the last neither." It wasn't said unkindly by Mrs O'Sullivan, which surprised me.

"I don't know what to do," I said, a single tear coursing down my cheek.

"Speak to the priest, child, he'll know what's what," said Mrs O'Sullivan, raising her eyebrows at the other, younger woman and clearing away the glass.

"Ok now, Biddy?' asked the younger woman. I nodded.

"Ye'll wait in here, Bridget, an' see the priest when he's finished," said Mrs O'Sullivan, adding almost as an after-thought, "D'ye want us to stay with ye?"

I shook my head, I couldn't bring myself to reply. I knew that as soon as the older lady was out of the room and back with the other parishioners, my secret would be halfway round Templemore before lunchtime.

The women left and I stared blankly at the stone wall.

Some time later the heavy wooden door creaked open and

the priest came in. He coughed as he entered and I looked away, not wanting to show him my face, which now blushed scarlet.

Father Connor pulled a chair to me after taking off his vestments, folding them away in a great chest filled with brightly coloured robes.

"I hope you've not been a naughty girl?" he began. I looked down at my bump.

Then a rush of rage hit me. A rising tide of anger swept through me. I hadn't been a naughty girl. I'd done nothing wrong yet I was being judged for it. I felt a protective surge of adrenaline, and so I turned to the father and spoke clearly: "My bump is proof enough for ye, but not of my own sins."

"What on earth d'ye mean by that, child?" exclaimed the priest.

"It was my brother Robert who did this. He – he forced himself upon me. There was nothing I could do, Father. He made this baby ye see here."

I knew that, to the priest, I would sound weak, but I was also determined not to lie in a holy place. There'd been enough lying already.

The priest sucked in his teeth. "Now, Bridget, why would you say such a wicked thing? Your brother is a decent man, that which ye have told me cannot be. He takes the collection box round every Sunday."

I stared at him in disbelief. Everyone in the town knew about Robert's 'tough man' behaviour, his nights carousing in the pubs. How could the priest think that because he attended Mass and took round the collection box, that would somehow forgive him his many sins outside of the church? The hypocrisy took my breath away.

"Father, ye have to believe me. It was Robert who did this, my own brother, and it is his sin not mine. Ye know he has a temper, he is a wilful, wicked man, for all that he helps ye at Mass," I implored.

The priest would not look me in the eyes. His stubborn refusal to acknowledge the truth of what I was saying snapped something inside me. I finally found my voice, my rage. I jumped up off the chair and stood facing the man who, I suddenly realised, held my fate, and that of my unborn child, in his hands.

If he didn't believe me, this baby was lost to me. I stared at him, my look must've been that of a wild woman, an impassioned and furious mother-to-be. In that moment I felt a surge of power, a need to be heard and to fight for my unborn child.

"I tell ye nothing but the truth. This baby inside me is a product of wickedness, but it is also one of God's creatures, and it deserves to be born in love, to be mine to raise as I see fit." I could hardly believe I could be so bold in standing up to the spiritual head of our parish. My tone changed. I softened, knowing I had to find a way for this man, this arrogant man, to hear what I was saying, to hear the truth that I laid now in front of him.

"I beg ye Father, listen to me. It was my brother Robert. He came in drunk one night and —"

"Stop! I've heard enough of your nasty little lies. What malice is this from ye, Bridget? How can ye say such wicked things in the sight of God, in His Holy church? You've committed a terrible sin, Bridget, a terrible sin."

I stood, silent, mouthing words that wouldn't come out. Every girl knew from an early age that conceiving a child out of wedlock was forbidden. I had wanted to erase the experience Robert had forced on me from my mind and soul, yet I couldn't regret this baby inside me. Somehow I saw this child as something separate from Robert's wickedness, almost as if the two were unrelated. I didn't question my feelings, I just knew at that moment that I wanted to bring up my child myself. I wanted to suckle him or her, change the wet nappies and feel a pudgy hand holding mine. I was desperate for someone to love – and to be loved. The priest's reaction told me that this was becoming an impossible dream. I moaned as the reality of my situation hit me, perhaps for the first time. I would be condemned in Templemore. I was now a 'disgrace', a loose woman. I would never be able to marry after this. I would be shunned even though none of it was my fault.

I stumbled out of the church that had formed such a huge part of my life, and from that moment I never stepped foot inside it again.

I needed help, and I had no idea where to get it.

Instead of heading home, I marched off to the local doctor's surgery in the main street of Templemore, carrying my coat, my belly held proudly for all to see. I had nothing to hide now. Every woman in the village would probably know before sunset tonight that Biddy Larkin was 'in trouble'. I held my head high as I walked, acknowledging no-one, walking forward as if in to battle.

"So, Bridget, I see you have a ... difficult situation." Doctor Fitzpatrick, an elderly man with white hair and an ill-fitting suit, stared over his glasses at me. I nodded, mute.

"Let me check you over, make sure you're healthy for your... pregnancy."

It was as if the doctor didn't even want to say the word. My shame was complete.

I said nothing as he examined me.

"You're a bit pale, Bridget Larkin, so I'll prescribe some iron tablets. Take two a day until you feel a bit more sprightly, then drop it down to one a day."

I nodded.

I had been feeling tired and washed-out but I'd put it down to the restless sleep I'd experienced since Robert's attack, and my nightly cup of sherry that had, over the months, become two cups as I needed more of the alcohol to soothe me into dozing off.

Just as I was gathering up my coat to leave, the doctor, clicking his tongue, asked: "A lad from McCann Barracks was it?" He was referring to the naval barracks situated just on the outskirts of Templemore. Many local girls had fallen foul of the charms of the young men passing through there, except of course, for me.

I stared at him, unable to tell him the truth, which had been shot down so expertly by the priest.

"Well," sighed the doctor, "you won't be the first and surely not the last." He cleared his throat. "And I'll be speakin' to the priest, so I will, Bridget. You'll have to go to Roscrea, to the mother and baby home there. There's nothing else that can be done."

I blinked. Roscrea – even the name made me shudder.

"I can't go there, doctor I can't. They'll take my baby from me so they will. Ye have to help me," I stammered.

The doctor shook his head. "It's the only way, Bridget, the only way." He signalled towards the door for me to leave.

"But... but ye can't take my baby, I won't let ye," I howled. All at once, the barriers I'd erected around myself were broken by my wail as I begged this man to save my child. "Please, doctor, please help me..."

He looked at me, not unkindly, then stood up, placed a hand on the small of my back and led me out to the waiting room.

Several people sitting on the wooden chairs lining one wall of the cottage were now watching us. I let myself be guided out, feeling like a prisoner being led to the gallows. Inside my heart was breaking. They were going to take my baby from me, and there was nothing I could do about it.

Back at home that night, Robert came in glowering as usual, and made it clear he wanted to talk to me. I wiped down my hands on Mam's old apron, and came to the kitchen table where he was sitting, his hands locked together on the surface, his frown sending shivers of fear down my spine.

"The Father has spoken to me today. I thought you'd put on weight but I had no idea...no idea of what you've done."

I gagged. I'm goin' to be sick, I can't bear this, this hypocrisy, I thought to myself, keeping my eyes cast down like a true penitent so he couldn't see the rebellious anger in my eyes.

"You've brought shame on this family, shame d'ye hear me? I told the priest what I'd suspected for a while now, that ye sleep around with any man who asks ye. I knew ye were nothin' but a whore after ye disgraced yourself with that Bill. Now this..."

It was pointless me saying anything. I knew if I so much as raised my voice to accuse him of his own crime then I would be beaten black and blue, and it might even give him the excuse he wanted to force himself upon me again. I had my child to protect now, and my maternal instinct proved greater than my revulsion at what Robert was saying.

Surely he couldn't believe that I'd slept around? Or was all of this his way of not accepting his own behaviour, how he raped me and left me pregnant? Surely he must know what he'd done? How could he not?

"I told the priest I wanted ye out of this house, out of Templemore and out of Ireland. I have no sister now. You've ruined yourself with your loose ways, and you've ruined our family name. From now on, you're dead to me. You're a bad girl. Ya won't be welcome at Mass or in this house again. Ye'll be leavin' for Roscrea in two days and until then I won't be sayin' another word to ye. Ye won't be returnin' back here, *Bad Biddy*. Templemore is no longer your home."

With that he stood up, ran his hand through his oily hair and pulled out his tobacco.

"I don't want to see ye. Get out of my sight."

Slowly, with as much dignity as I could muster, I stood up. I turned round and made my way up the stairs, without saying a single word to defend myself.

I pulled my door shut behind me and leaned against it, my eyes closing, my breathing becoming quieter. I had no idea what lay in store for me. I had no clue as to what he had planned. Where would I go if I couldn't come home? And yet even though the thought of leaving chilled me, at that moment I couldn't be upset about not seeing Robert, or the priest or the gossiping women of the town, again. I held my hands over my belly, feeling the strong kick of the infant inside me.

CHAPTER 10
A LABOUR OF LOVE
January 1951

"Push, Biddy, PUSH!" The nun shook her head, her lips pursed with distaste.

"Oh Holy Mother of God!" I shouted, in pain and fear as a contraction ripped through me. Another surge engulfed my trembling body, then another. I was lying on a bed in a separate room, away from the dormitories we girls shared, surrounded by three of the nuns from the Sisters of the Sacred Heart of Jesus and Mary, which ran the Sean Ross Abbey Home in Roscrea, County Tipperary. The home was part of the Sacred Heart Adoption Society's network, which took the babies of unmarried girls and, for large donation fees, gave them up for adoption to rich American families.

"You're going to have to work harder than that, Bridget Larkin. There's a reason this is called labour, now push again."

I stared wildly up at Sister Immaculata, wearing her long, black habit and veil over her starched white coif. Her face was hidden in the shadow cast by the overhead light.

Other than the three sisters, I was utterly alone, with no family and no friends beside me. There was no pain relief given, no midwife or doctor present.

Whatever happened was God's will, or so I was told by Sister Conrad, a pale-faced older nun who muttered prayers under her breath through my ordeal.

Many mothers and babies died here. We all knew the stories handed down between each 'inmate'. There were bramble-covered crosses on the land surrounding the home, with the names of those unfortunate girls who lost their lives giving birth. I prayed with a kind of manic fervour that I would not be one of them.

It was the start of 1951, as bleak and as cold a start to any year that I could remember. I had been at the mother and baby home for more than four months before the birth of my child. Every day had been like a fresh punishment in this dour, imposing place. Once a country house, the two-storey building was now home to the county's 'shameful' unmarried mothers – women like me who had been abandoned, left to fend for themselves as their bellies swelled with their disgrace. It was a cold place, with high ceilings and austere furnishings, adorned only with devotional statues and images.

Each morning before dawn we were all awakened by a nun, and together we traipsed into the chapel for Mass, the first prayers of the new day, after which we were led in silence to a meagre breakfast of porridge. The duties of our day were set before us by the nuns in attendance, and mine were usually in the steaming, broiling laundry room. Throughout the late stages of my pregnancy I was expected to haul dirty washing – nuns' habits, bed sheets and linen – into the great vats of boiling water. Once dredged inside, I would have to stir them round, my face red and my body sweating with the heat and effort involved. Carefully, trying not to burn ourselves, we would have to take the heavy, wet material out to be scrubbed clean with sweet-smelling soap, our soggy hair falling on our faces, our backs aching with the workload. Then mid-morning we'd be led out again, like a flock of submissive sheep, back to chapel for morning prayers.

Most of the time I was too exhausted to take any of the service in. My pregnancy was advanced and my body hurt all the time. The baby kicked furiously with the heat and I sighed my way through each day, thinking only of the small respite each evening brought.

"PUSH Bridget, you need to try harder than that!" Sister Hildegarde glared at me through her glasses, her slight frame belying the ferocity of her disapproval.

"Jaysus Christ, I'm dying! This baby will kill me!" I shrieked. I was terrified. No-one had told me anything about this pain. I was completely unprepared.

"We won't have language like that in here, you deserve to be whipped!" retorted the sister, her face devoid of any human warmth.

"This is your punishment for your sins, you should embrace it and thank the Lord for His purification."

I cried out again. Sister Immaculata leaned in. The large cross that hung from her habit swung forward. Her voice was soft as she spoke but her words chilled me.

"Now Bridget, stop your moaning! It's your own fault, ye deserve no better."

Sister Hildegarde added: "You won't get any sympathy here," as the contractions engulfed me again.

Now my body took over, swell after swell rolled over me until a final push and my baby slid from me. I looked up. My thighs, shaking in the aftermath of the birth, were coated with blood and slick with sweat. Sister Immaculata held a dark-haired infant in her arms: my baby.

"It's a boy, and he looks healthy and strong. He's a gift from God for a good Catholic family," was all she said.

"Let me hold him," I begged, reaching out my arms. They ached for him, as if they'd done the work of expelling him. The sister wiped him down and he started to wriggle, letting out a loud wail. Tears sprung to my eyes. My son – I will meet my son at last.

"Give him to me," I said, still reaching for him.

Sister Immaculata handed my baby to the youngest of the nuns, Sister Annunciata, who wrapped him in a pristine white blanket. She turned to look at me, her face blank. The baby howled again.

"Let me hold him, please Sister Annunciata, just for a moment," I urged. My heart was full of love and I sniffed the air, hoping to catch his baby smell, that indefinable primal bond of flesh and blood that I remembered from my mother's room after she'd given birth to Philomena.

But the nun didn't come to my bedside. She didn't hand the snuffling bundle of warmth to me. Instead, she turned away and walked out of the room, the door slamming shut behind her. I scrabbled up on the bed.

"Come back. No, no, noo. Come back. I want to hold my son!" I was frantic, clawing my way off the sheets. The two remaining sisters ran to me, holding me down so I couldn't drag my bleeding body out of that room. I wrestled with them, spitting with fury, demanding to see my child.

"Calm down, Bridget, calm down. There's nothing to be done. You can't see him till you're obedient."

I heard the words but they didn't make sense. My head swam.

I could feel nothing, see nothing, except the dark head of my baby being taken away from me.

My voice was cracked but still I shouted: "Bring him back, bring me my baby, I want my baby."

"When you're calm and quiet, ye can see him but not before. He's not your baby any longer, Bridget Larkin. He'll be someone else's little boy soon so you'd better get used to the idea, child." I looked up at Sister Immaculata.

"He's mine. He'll always be mine. God will see your sin, He'll see what ya do to us here, and he'll judge ye," I spat.

The sister only smiled. "We'll see, missy, we'll see about that won't we? Now let's clean you up."

In the silence that followed, my sadness seemed to break me. I burst into sobs, my whole body heaving with the agony of not holding my newborn.

I had arrived at the home on a drizzly dark afternoon at the start of September 1950. I'd been picked up from home by the Moral Welfare Officer, a young woman named Miss Agnes McKenna, and the priest. No-one came to see me off, not even my friend Kate, though I'd hoped she might slip away. Perhaps my shame was too much even for her, or, most likely, she'd been told by her pa to stay away from me. I would never know for sure.

My brother Robert got up that morning and left for work at dawn without saying a word. I was the local loose woman, 'Bad Biddy' now, and so not one person from the neighbourhood I'd lived in all my life came to say goodbye. I knew then, deep in my heart, I'd never be able to return. I was branded a 'whore'. There was nothing left for me there. I'd packed a few items in my small suitcase. A change of clothes, hairbrush and the small plastic ring, my only reminder of my passionate love for Bill. I sat in the back seat of the car and stared directly ahead of me. I didn't look at the familiar streets, the rows of houses and shops, the steeple of the church. I looked ahead, blind to everything, holding my stomach as if to reassure the baby – and perhaps myself.

Even the name Roscrea struck fear into the local girls. It was known as a severe place. A place where sins were punished. I was entirely alone in carrying my family's darkest secret. As Roscrea was in County Tipperary, the drive was not a long one, being only 18 miles away, yet it was the longest trip of my life so far. I stared at the wipers as they scraped along the windscreen; by now torrential rain stung the glass pane and visibility was poor as we drove through the winding country lanes.

At the entrance was a metal arch with the name of the establishment written along it. I shivered at the sight of it. We drove slowly down a long, gravel drive, surrounded by lush, green land, no doubt owned by the institution. The home was once a country estate, with a large, imposing front door.

Getting out of the car, the Moral Welfare Officer touched my arm briefly, as if in some way trying to give me reassurance.

"You will get over this and soon forget about it," she said, but I knew in my soul that was a lie and this was something I would never, ever forget. I felt as small as a mouse standing in front of it, backed by my keepers.

The bell clanged through the house, then the door was opened by a nun in black garments. She ushered us into a room at the back of the house that looked onto gardens. A clock ticked on the mantelpiece. For minutes that stretched like hours we sat waiting, until at last the door opened and a tall woman walked in, her robes following in her wake.

"Hello, I am Sister Barbara, Superioress of Sean Ross Abbey, and you are Bridget, I presume?"

I nodded, keeping my eyes fixed on my hands, held in my lap.

"Well Bridget, I'd like you to go with Sister Marie-Therese here. She'll show you where you'll be staying and what your duties are."

She gestured to a younger-looking nun with a plain face who had slipped into the room without a sound. I stood up and walked from that room without speaking a word. The door shut behind me and I followed the nun up the grand staircase towards the large alabaster figure of Our Lady that stood watching our ascent. I crossed myself, whispering a blessing, though the words felt meaningless in this cold, austere building.

The nun took me to a long room with beds lining each side. There must have been 20 beds in there at least, and she directed me to one of them. A wooden chair beside the bedhead acted as a small table and I unpacked my possessions, conscious of the silence that seemed to stifle the air in there.

"You'll start your chores today. The sisters are expectin' ye down in the laundry. Ye can take an apron from the end cupboard and follow me if ye will."

Clutching the cotton garment, I followed the nun again, our heeled shoes tapping on the shining clean floor.

The laundry was in the bowels of the building and the first thing that hit me was the heat of the steam, then the noise. Here, at least, there was life. Girls chatted and were shushed by prim-faced nuns in black habits. A giant cross hung on the wall, with Jesus, flayed and dying, imposed upon it. Water sloshed, garments were scrubbed, the whole place had the feel of a watery hell, but I instantly preferred it to the lack of sound above-stairs.

I tied the apron around my large waist and looked around for my next instruction.

"Over here, ye can come an' help me with these sheets. They're bloody killin' me so they are." The girl smiled and waved me over. She had red curly hair and a belly bigger than mine.

"Y'must be due soon?" I guessed, grabbing one end of the soaking-wet fabric.

"Jaysus, it can't come a day too soon. Those nuns are more like devils in skirts, making us work when we're fit to drop. My name's Orla by the way, what's yours?"

"Bridget," I answered. "Come here. Let me take that, ye'll do yourself an injury trying to carry that, it's far too heavy."

I dragged the sheet from her otherwise small frame, and she rolled her eyes heavenwards.

"How long have ye been here?" I asked, happy to be chatting to someone.

"Ach, nearly two months now. My family got rid of me as soon as I started showing, now they won't have me back so I'm stuck here for the whole three years." Orla sighed, mopping her brow.

"What d'ye mean, three years?" I was looking at her, puzzled.

She snorted, a laugh without mirth. "Don't ye know, that's the deal? We have our babies here. They're adopted away to America or overseas and then, if our families haven't the money to bail us out, the £100 the Catholic Church wants for releasing us, then we have to stay and work for three years for free. Slave labour I call it," huffed Orla.

"Three years?" I said stupidly, as if the words didn't make sense. I knew that no-one would bail me out. I knew no-one would come for me. Robert had said he wanted me out of Templemore for good. Perhaps this was what he meant.

My face must've registered my shock, as Orla put her hand on my shoulder.

"Ye'll get used to it, ye have to…." At that moment one of the nuns marched over and began admonishing us for our tardiness.

That night, exhausted after a day spent washing, scrubbing and squeezing linens through one of the great mangles, I lay on my side, holding the only thing in life, apart from my baby, that was dear to me.

The pink plastic ring was gaudy and cheap. It had no monetary value, yet even the sight of it still made my heart beat faster. I conjured up Bill's face in my mind, though the image had faded over the months. Even though he'd let me down, left me alone in Ireland, it wasn't Bill's fault I was in here. He wasn't the father of my child, but I wished he had been, and in thinking that, I knew myself to be a sinner, just as the nuns told me I was. I was outside of God's law in wanting to have lain with my sweetheart. I wished I had felt his heart thump against mine, the feel of his naked skin, his kiss on my mouth, throat, neck… I was doing penance for my brother's crime – yet more than ever I wished it had been Bill's. And here I was, stuck washing the nuns' stinking robes as I wished and waited for the day I'd hold my baby in my arms. I hated them for their piety and their strict moral codes. Underneath their crosses and their robes were women made of flesh like me. How could the love of a woman for a man be sinful? How could the nuns be nearer to God when all they practiced was cruelty?

I had finally given birth to my son that morning of January 1951, yet it was now afternoon and I hadn't even held him, hadn't kissed his fuzzy head or marvelled at his tiny fingers and toes. Even that pleasure had been denied me.

The sound of babies crying came from the nursery at the end of a long hallway, and out of the din I tried to find the noise made by my own child. But I couldn't tell, I couldn't pick out my own child and the horror of that seeded in my mind, perhaps laying waste to my sanity in the years to come.

Some of the girls, especially Orla, had asked me about the father of my baby, but I was so lacking in faith that they'd believe me that I wouldn't answer, and only nodded when they said it must've been a local lad getting me in 'trouble'.

One day, not long before the birth, as I had dragged a heavy sack of coal from the scullery to the Mother Superior's office, one of the nuns had seen the look of revolt on my face.

"If ye play with fire, ye must expect to get burnt," she'd said, as she walked past me, a small smile playing on her lips. If I could've instructed hell's fire to burn the place to cinders at that moment, I would've done so without a second thought because I knew she wasn't alluding to the coal. The blame, the moral defect, was considered to be mine, and mine alone. When I asked God how this could be, I received only silence in reply.

CHAPTER 11
EXILED TO ENGLAND

"Sign here, Bridget please."

I stared at the crisp white document laid out on Mother Superior Sister Barbara's desk.

"You want me to sign away my baby?"

"Of course." The woman tutted as if I was keeping her from some more important task. "You cannot look after this child, and after what you said to Sister Hildegarde yesterday, it is better for all concerned if you leave this place, and leave your child to be cared for by those who can do it properly. You are not well, Bridget. You need to go away for treatment. We don't keep lunatics here. Now, waste no more of my time, please. Sign here." Sister Barbara pointed to the dotted line at the end of the sheet of paper, underneath the words that would separate me from my child forever.

I knew why this was happening so suddenly – and why I was being branded insane. Usually girls stayed for those three years working at the abbey home, being allowed an hour a day to see their child until their adoption, which for most was worth the scourge of their free labour. But this was being denied me, and all because I had dared to shout the truth at one of these nuns, whose displeasure was like a canker in their souls.

Only five days after giving birth, after which time I'd only seen my beautiful baby Kieran a handful of times, I was told it was time for me to start work again in the laundry. My breasts leaked milk and my body was still sore and bruised, making it painful to walk, but disobedience was not tolerated, and before I knew it I was back in the basement, dredging sheets from the vats and crying with sheer exhaustion.

The other girls, some of whom had become friends, were sympathetic, but they had received the same treatment themselves. Orla had been back working a week after her little girl Dara (a name which meant 'kindness') was born, shortly after I arrived. Her little one was four months old now, with the same fiery red curls as her mammy. There was also Faith, who had given birth to a boy she'd named Patrick, or Paddy as we called him, after Ireland's best-known saint, and Ciara, who was about to pop any moment. She was carrying her baby high so we were all convinced it'd be a boy!

Ciara was the bravest of the four of us. She made no bones about hating the home, but she did it without ever drooping her head. She looked the hated nuns square in the face, she always spoke back, and we'd lost count of the number of penances Ciara had to do, but none of it took the sharp glint out of her eye. She had sworn she would go to America after this, and would never return to her 'stinkin' home in nearby Roscrea. She declared that she hated Ireland, but most of all she hated the boy she'd fallen for, who'd upped and left after she told him she was pregnant. I couldn't see anything in life bringing down Ciara, and perhaps it was her influence that made me break the home rules so flagrantly.

It was the sixth day after giving birth, and we were working and cursing when Sister Hildegarde hurried into the basement. She whispered to the nun overseeing our work, and Ciara said: "Here we go, what now? If it's Sister Hildegarde then we're in trouble."

The nun was known for her sternness and we feared and loathed her in equal measure. She seemed to take great delight in telling us we were destined for hell unless we repented our sinful ways.

The sister looked over at Orla, whose head was bent as she bundled up the dirty clothing. In that moment, I knew that Dara was being taken.

Orla looked up and I caught her gaze. At first she looked confused, then the penny dropped. She froze, dropping the fabric to the floor. Sister Hildegarde marched out, and this time, against the rules, I ran after her.

"Tell me what's happening? You're taking Dara aren't ye? Someone's coming to adopt her aren't they? And then she's supposed to stay for three years, for three bloody years!" I shouted as I ran. The nun walked faster and when I caught up with her I was panting with exertion. I grabbed her bony arm.

"Get your hands off me, Bridget Larkin. I won't have a sinner such as yourself touch me. Get back to work immediately."

"No!" I said, blocking her way. "Tell me what's happening now. Orla might be too good by not asking, but I'm not."

"No," sneered the sister, "you're not. I know all about ye and your wickedness."

Her voice was like a hiss. "I know the lies you've told, God help your soul. I know ye blamed your brother for your troubles, of all the terrible things to say, when it was your morals that failed."

I stepped back as if I'd been struck. "I told the truth, sister. My brother raped me, so he did. He was drunk and he forced himself onto me, and my baby boy Kieran is the result of that. I didn't lie. The only liars in this place are you and your band of nuns." I barely drew breath. "You're a disgrace to the church. You're heartless. Ye take our children and force us to

work. Ye won't let us see them for more than an hour a day…"
I broke down into sobs.

By now a crowd of girls and nuns surrounded us.

The people parted and the Mother Superior stood in front of me. Her face was like thunder, and her voice, when it came, was cold as ice.

"Bridget, you will get back to work immediately. I will decide your punishment for this later. You will come and see me tomorrow, without fail."

My anger crumbled. I started at the sea of faces around me, feeling suddenly foolish. "Yes, Mother Superior," I said, gulping down my distress. Wiping the tears from my face I ran off, desperate now to get away, the women from the laundry drifting back behind me. Sister Hildegarde's words beat against my brain. Why didn't they believe me? I couldn't answer that, except to know that my voice counted for little in Ireland at that time. Us women were wives and daughters, sisters or whores, all of our relationships defined by the men and the church that controlled us.

I looked around but Orla was missing. So I had been right. Dara was being taken away. Poor Orla, poor, poor Orla. For a moment I forgot my own sorrows.

I didn't care what punishment would be meted out to me, instead I felt the pain that my friend must have been feeling deep in my soul. To give birth to a child then to have that little person, that part of your own heart, taken away so brutally. Was there anything more painful?

My small rebellion was the reason I was standing in the Mother Superior's office the next morning. It was a freezing cold January day despite the fire glowing in the grate. At least I had the warmth of the laundry to escape to after this, or so I thought to myself.

The clock ticked its doleful sound. The piece of paper I had to sign lay on the desk in front of me. Sister Barbara held out a pen. It read: "I relinquish full claim forever to my child and surrender him to Sister Barbara, Superioress of Sean Ross Abbey. The purpose is to enable Sister Barbara to make my child available for adoption to any person she considers fit and proper, inside or outside the state. I further undertake never to attempt to see, interfere with, or make any claim to the said child at any future time."

"You have to sign this, Bridget," said Sister Barbara calmly. "There is no other way left for you now. Yesterday's events convinced me that we cannot help you here. You are mentally ill, my child, and not fit to be a mother, not even for the time you are allowed to be while you work here.

"I have come to the decision, upon speaking to your brother Robert, who I believe is the head of your family now, that you are best off in an asylum."

"An asylum… ye can't mean it, Mother Superior," I protested. "But I'm telling the truth about Robert. Why won't any of ye believe me?" I was begging, pleading with her.

Her face was stony, her lips pressed together in a thin, mean line. "Arrangements have been made. You leave today for England for a hospital for the mentally unwell. We cannot have you here, upsetting the sisters and creating a disturbance. Your brother has said very clearly that it is best for you to start a new life across the water, and I agree. That is my final word on the subject. As soon as you have signed this you can see Kieran for the final time."

So even my love for my son had become a bargaining tool. I was dumbfounded, but I knew I was being sent away for a reason – because the scandal was so great that my community would never have me back. And darker reasons existed, no doubt. If I was ever believed, Robert would be charged with rape and incest. No, I saw it plain as day, there was no way he would let that happen and so I had been branded 'insane' and now I would be packed off on a steam ferry to England.

A convenient exit for all concerned – except me and my beautiful boy. Each night at the home, I had wept for the inevitable loss of him as each day brought it closer and closer to the moment he would be adopted, and I would be his mother no more. I knew my outburst had served only to bring the loss of my son closer, and the regret I felt was beyond anything I'd suffered till then.

Each evening the nuns made me express my milk to feed to him. Each day I was allowed the one short hour with him after my work was done, and it wasn't nearly enough. I had wept for the knowledge that one day soon I would have to give him up – and that day had come sooner than anyone could've predicted.

I saw clearly then I had no choice. If I wanted to cuddle my little newborn, cover him in kisses and sing him a lullaby for the very last time, then I had to sign.

I took the pen, my hand shaking, and scribbled my name at the bottom. A single tear splashed onto the page as I finished staining the ink, a permanent record of this unwanted, barbaric act.

"Good, Bridget. You see, you can be obedient. Now you can go to see the child, but you leave in two hours."

I ran from her office, making sure I banged the door hard on my way out. I raced towards the nursery, a long, narrow building at the back of the home.

"Get out of my way!" I shouted as I went, bursting through the nursery door without knocking.

"What in the name of heaven…" exclaimed one of the nuns. I ignored her.

Frantically I looked around for Kieran. He was lying in one of the cots, his face bunched up, looking for all the world like he was about to scream his own anger at the terrible parting we were being forced into.

"Come here my littl' darlin', come here, my beautiful boy," I crooned as I lifted him out of his cot. His face immediately relaxed and he turned his head to me, his mouth rooting for my milk.

Without thinking, I sat down and unfastened my apron, holding him against me as he started to suckle.

"What do ye think you're doing?" shrieked Sister Annunciata, but I ignored her, planting kisses on my son's head as he nuzzled against me and humming a lullaby I'd heard my mammy sing to us as children. When he'd had his fill I moved him to my other breast and sat watching him in wonder as he latched on – as if this was the most natural thing in the world, which of course it was.

"That's all I can give ye, Kieran, because the nuns are taking me away from ye.

D'ye hear me, my darlin', they're sending me away from ye so I need ye to hear this, and keep it locked inside ye forever so that when you're older you'll know that ye were loved by your mammy.

"You'll always be my baby boy. Whoever takes ye home, whoever looks after ye and changes your clouts and tickles your tummy, I loved ye first. I'll miss ye so much. I'll miss ye." Tears threatened to fall again. At that point two nuns walked up.

"Bridget," said one of them kindly, "Bridget, it's time for you to go. It's better for the baby if you don't make a fuss. You must go now and pack your things. The car will be here soon." I looked up and she must've seen the look of bleak horror on my face. "Give me more time – please," I begged. "Mother Superior said I had two hours."

The nun shook her head, her face filled with sorrow. There was kindness in her touch as she slowly, firmly, eased Kieran out of my arms, leaving them suddenly weightless as if made of paper.

"It's time to go. Kieran will be looked after. He'll be safe here with us. Now go, don't look back Bridget, just go."

Several hours later, I stood on the brow of the steam ferry that chugged across the channel to England. The sky was already darkening above the grey, churning waves and I stood, oblivious to the cold and the spray and I wept until I could weep no longer. My whole body and heart yearned for my son, any sorrow I had felt until this point in my life was as nothing compared with the agony that gripped me now. I didn't know how I was going to physically bear it, how I could carry on living without him. I hadn't looked back at Ireland's shoreline as we left Rosslare Harbour. I didn't want to see my homeland ever again, the land that had betrayed me, had hurt me so deeply, though at least I would be free of Robert, free of the nuns but I knew the memories would always haunt me. Perhaps a new life in England would save me from my memories and the torments they gave me?

CHAPTER 12
SEARCHING FOR PEACE

It was pitch black when the car that had met me at Pembroke arrived in the city of Manchester. I barely looked out of the window. I was cold, exhausted, hungry and hurting. My birth wounds had barely had a chance to heal and, while my breasts continued to leak the milk that was no longer needed, my heart felt like it had frozen solid in my chest. The car pulled up in front of an impressive building, the largest I'd ever seen in my life, with columns and a clock tower that loomed against the darkness. The sign above the entrance said: "Manchester Royal Infirmary and Lunatic Asylum". Just in case we patients were in any doubt about our mental state.

Clutching my suitcase I was led into one of the wards, a large, long room with high ceilings, lined with metal beds. A nurse in starched apron and headdress looked me up and down, and said, "Follow me." We walked in silence until we reached one of the empty beds.

Sinking down onto it, I lay my head on the pillow, folding my body into the foetal position. Somebody close by was snoring. A woman with straggly white hair hummed a tune to herself as she sat bolt upright in her bed, while the person next to me was folded up, rather like myself, under the blankets. I didn't dare move. I didn't dare say a word. I was far from home. I was grieving for my baby. I was terrified of the asylum and what the next day might bring.

The following days were lost in a blur of medication and the visits of various doctors and nurses who proceeded to look me up and down with grave expressions. Our iron beds were lined up regimentally along one crumbling wall. We had no cabinets, nowhere to put precious things, no privacy from each other. Overnight I heard every grunt and groan from the inmates, every whispered rant, every muffled prayer. Each ward had a matron who oversaw the routine, and every day was the same, starting with early rising, the drugs trolley then hours of intense, floating boredom until supper, the last drug round of the day and lights out.

My neighbour usually stayed under her bedding, huddled into herself, refusing to eat, wash or dress. The elderly woman with white hair howled like a strange animal from time to time, and other patients staggered around the ward, all dressed in the same hospital robes and slippers.

Men were separated from women, but many times at night as I lay sleepless, the on-duty nurse asleep at her station, I saw one of the male patients, a stocky menacing-looking man in his fifties, standing at the ward entrance, watching us. I mentioned it to one of the inmates, a woman in her forties with thick lustrous dark hair and a wild expression and she shushed me, a look of fear on her face: "Don't tell the nurse, or he'll know. He's a bad one, a bad one Biddy." Then she scuttled off.

Each morning the nurses did the drug rounds, and I'd been swallowing mine without thinking. But one day I stopped, only pretending to take them, and hiding the white pills inside the cabinet next to my bed. I hated the feeling of being woozy all day, but that wasn't the only reason. As the days passed, my feelings of despair increased. My body and soul ached for the child I'd given up, my guilt at signing the adoption papers ate away at me. I was looking for a way out, one that would cause the minimum of fuss.

"Come on love, we're going down for your treatment," said the nurse standing over my bed. A solid-built woman in her forties, she helped me up and half dragged me to a waiting wheelchair.

"I don't need to sit in that thing!" I exclaimed.

"Oh just enjoy the rest, come on, that's it," she encouraged as I settled into it.

"But where are we goin'?" I asked.

"For your treatment, as I said." She spoke brusquely, in a voice that brooked no argument.

She wheeled me down a series of long corridors and into a different ward. People were lying in beds but no-one was moving. The sight struck me as very odd.

"What's the matter with those unfortunates?" I asked, trying to turn my head to look at them, but the nurse sped up.

"Nothing for you to worry about, lovey."

We pulled up inside a smaller room. A single bed stood in the middle, with leather straps on either side of the head and feet.

"What's this?" I stammered, trying to get myself up out of the wheelchair.

Suddenly I was flanked on both sides by two male attendants in surgical scrubs.

"Bridget, we're trying to help you. Will you please stop struggling and listen to me."

I stared up at her. My heart was pounding, this didn't feel right, not at all.

"What's that thing there. I'm not getting' on that bed…"

"We're going to give you something called Electric Convulsive Therapy, or ECT as it's known. Do you know what that is,

Bridget?" said the nurse, who was clearly a senior figure in the hospital.

I shook my head.

"It's a treatment where we use a series of small electric shocks to reset your brain. You do want to get better don't you?"

As she spoke I felt the tears rolling down my face. I wasn't sure I did want to get better. A depression had settled onto me since arriving in Manchester. I didn't want to sleep or eat. I felt my life wasn't worth living, and that perhaps I really was as 'bad' as everyone told me I was. Without family or friends, I was alone in a strange place surrounded by stranger people. No-one listened to me. No-one cared for me. In truth, I wanted to die.

I turned my face away.

"Help her up, please," said the nurse to the men. They pulled me out of the chair and led me to the bed where I let myself be laid down, and the straps tied to my wrists and ankles.

A great machine was wheeled closer to the bed. I shut my eyes. Something was placed on my head.

"What you can feel is two electrodes. They'll send an electric pulse through your brain. It'll be very quick but it will cause you to have a seizure."

"What d'ye mean, a seizure?" I felt pure terror.

"Don't worry Bridget, we know what we're doing, now try to relax."

I was about to reply when the machine started buzzing. The room swayed in front of my eyes and then everything went black.

"Come on now, Bridget, wake up." I heard the nurse's voice as if from far away.

My eyes opened, I was lying on my side, my body felt strange.

I was in that same room the nurse pushed me through earlier. I tried to speak but words failed me.

My head was buzzing, but I felt oddly peaceful and quite content to stay where I was. The nurse bustled round me. I had no idea how long I'd lain there, and I really didn't care. Eventually I was wheeled back to my bed where I lay for several more days before the same process happened again, and again. I don't know how many treatments I was subjected to, but each one left me feeling more and more disconnected from everyone and everything around me.

As life went on around me, I was suspended in a woozy haze, with one day bleeding into another. I lay on the metal bed, not knowing what was real and what was imagined as my mind tried to find comfort from that inhuman regime. I sometimes pictured the church steeple opposite our house in Templemore, the russet autumn leaves, and the dimpled face of Philomena. I could often smell her hair, feel her little body leaning against me in the bed and then my arms would encircle the milky-scented bundle of baby Kieran. I heard Bill's honeyed voice whispering, "I'm coming for ye Biddy, wait for me." Once I saw Mam's face, as it used to be when I was young, without the ravages of booze and sadness. She was smiling softly and saying, "There now, my Biddy, don't ye cry, Mammy's here." And in between there were the nightmares: Patrick's heavy, lolling tongue, Robert's staring eyes boring into me, ravaging me. I could do nothing to stop the images that floated into my mind. My mind, like my body, was no longer my own; my life was nothing.

When the day finally came to discharge me, I made sure I hid the stash of pills I'd saved up over the weeks in my suitcase. I don't know if it was the electric shock therapy, the shock of leaving Ireland or the loss of my child, but at some point in the asylum I'd decided I would end it all as soon as I was out and free to put my plan into action.

"Goodbye, Bridget," said the ward matron stiffly, her apron as starched as her temperament.

I nodded my response, hiding my eagerness to be free of that place, though my head was ringing with the after-effects of my treatments. I thought of my stash of pills and smiled.

"That's good, Bridget, put a happy face on and good luck to you." The matron walked me along the corridor, having no notion of my plan to end it all, no idea what I was plotting. I grimaced as I passed each ward, smelling the stench of disinfectant and faeces, the unwashed smell of some of the patients, the helpless, hopeless state of many of them. One woman, who had been inside the asylum for many years, whooped with joy in a manic kind of solidarity when she saw me leaving, her eyes shining, but just as quickly she stumbled away, distracted by something else.

Each step of mine took me away from that place. Each step took me to freedom, yet I was determined on my course of action.

Outside, a car waited for me, which I climbed inside, clutching my suitcase with its few contents.

Minutes later, we drew up outside a tenement building and the driver helped me out. He handed me a slip of paper with my new address, then, with a bashful smile, left me standing there, surrounded by the bustle of normal life, the sounds from the train station and the smoke from the chimneys. It took me a few moments to centre myself, gather my faculties enough to step forward to look for my new abode. In the end I asked a nearby flower seller who handed me a small posy of early violets.

"Don't look so sad, luvvie, Spring is around the corner," she cackled, showing a mouth filled with blackened teeth.

I thanked her and walked on, my hands gripping the posy like they were a lifeline, saving me from drowning. I felt disorientated. My head swam with the sights and sounds that seemed so exaggerated, so vividly real. Not only had I spent the last few weeks in a hospital bed, I had never travelled outside of my hometown before arriving in Manchester, and the experience of being somewhere wholly new and unknown to me was as thrilling as it was frightening. By the time I found the room, located my key from the landlady who lived on the ground floor of the rather miserable-looking building, I felt faint and more than a little tired.

"You don't look well, petal," remarked the woman as I thanked her for the key. She was a portly looking matron with white hair scraped back off her face and a not-unfriendly face.

"I'm just a little tired, thank you." I stumbled over my words in my increasing desperation to get into my own room and lock the door behind me.

Hands shaking, I gripped the bannister and pulled myself up the flight of stairs. The lock shuddered as I turned the key and then I was inside. There wasn't much to look at. A small iron bed stood in one corner with a sagging mattress and a pile of blankets, for which I felt grateful suddenly, to the point of tears.

There was a small fireplace with a wooden stool beside it and a bedpan. In the left corner was a small table, a single chair and a cooking ring to make my supper on. My stomach suddenly growled and I realised I had eaten little that day. I guessed that the rent for my tiny one-room bedsit had been paid for by the church while the money in my pocket, given to me by a stern-looking, suited man at the asylum, was from the poor fund that kept many a family going in those days. I would be expected to look for work within days, and knew the help would only ever be temporary. I needed to eat. Without another thought I went back out into the busy street amid the rumble of trains and the drunks and prostitutes hanging around Piccadilly. All at once, Manchester seemed to me a frightening and soulless place. I found a pie shop and bought myself a good dinner, then I spied a liquor store. Before I knew what I was doing, and after so many months of not touching a drop at Roscrea then at the asylum, I walked straight in and bought a bottle of gin. I wanted something to act quickly and potently when I carried out my planned suicide. I hastened back to the bedsit, trying to hide the bottle wrapped in brown paper under my coat. I felt a keen sense of shame as I half walked, half ran back to the safety of my room. My plan was monstrous. I knew that, and yet I knew I was entirely alone in the world. I had no-one to turn to and nowhere to go. I had no home except this dank room, looking even bleaker as the light started to fade.

I drank straight from the bottle, feeling the sharp tang of the alcohol hit my throat then deliver its balm. I ate half of my supper, preferring instead to drink away my sorrow and my loneliness.

I sat by the small window, listening to the sounds as evening fell, then into the night; people cat-calling to each other, shrieks and raucous laughter. I thought about everyone who I'd loved in my life, smiling as I recalled Philomena's girlish pouts when I tucked her up in her blankets at night, her determination to stay awake as I sang lullabies to her, how her eyes drooped as eventually sleep overcame her. I remembered Jimmie's grinning, cheeky face as he played yet another trick on Robert, his joyful laughter, the way he ruffled my hair even as a boy himself. Then Bill's face swam before me, his face close to mine as he kissed me, his searching hands touching my body, my desire making him laugh and throw me off him, teasing me, knowing I was his, body and soul. And my little baby Kieran. It was an agony to recall that last cuddle with him, but I forced myself to. I wanted his face to be the last in my mind before I took my own life.

The bottle was half-drunk now, I staggered to my suitcase and pulled out the pills which I washed down with more gin. As I swallowed, tears came to my eyes. I wiped them away, and looking round I realised my door was ajar. In my eagerness to open the bottle, I'd forgotten to shut my own door. It seemed so very far away from me now, so very distant. The room took on a hazy glow. My body was sinking to the floor and to me it felt like I was greeted by a bed of soft cushions rather than the bare floorboards underneath me. My sight faded, everything melted away until all that was left was the image of Christ's Bleeding Heart that used to sit in our kitchen, instead it wasn't Christ's head I saw but Kieran's, with one angelic finger pointed to his own heart – red, visceral, bleeding.

***

"Bridget, wake up, wake up. D'you hear me. Bridget, wake up now girl." Someone was shaking me, shouting in my ear.

I started and moaned as nausea hit me, my head pounding.

"What?!" I roared, then sank back into the bed I realised I was lying on. I was in a familiar place. It wasn't the bedsit. It wasn't back home in Ireland. It was the same asylum I'd left only hours earlier.

A matron I didn't recognise was the one who'd been shouting to wake me.

"What's happening?" I said as the urge to be sick mounted within me. I retched then leaned over the bed, puking on the floor.

"Now, now Bridget, what have you done to yourself?" The matron tutted before sending off another nurse for a kidney dish.

I tried to sit up but my body wouldn't cooperate and I flopped back onto the pillows.

"You're in a terrible mess, Bridget. Now why did you go and do something like that to yourself? Surely it wasn't worth the bother of ending up back in here?"

I knew she was trying to rouse me but I didn't care – it wasn't going to work. If it was possible, I felt even worse than I had the night before.

"Who found me?" was all I could say before doubling up to be sick again.

"You gave your landlady a great fright. She heard you moaning and groaning in your room, then crying and cursing and goodness knows what else. I doubt she'll have you back again. What were you thinking taking all that gin, Bridget?"

So they didn't know about the tablets. I decided it was best for me if I didn't mention those.

"I don't know, sister. My head's all muddled. I felt so sad, so very sad. I miss my baby…" My voice petered off. There was a moment's silence before I added: "But how did I end up back here?"

"You were admitted to the hospital and they decided you were a danger to yourself and sectioned you, so here you are. Back here with us."

The matron's voice softened: "It could've been so different for you, Bridget. You could've started again, made a life for yourself."

At that I broke down. I cried and wept as if I'd never stop, wondering if I would ever feel true happiness again.

CHAPTER 13
LOVERS REUNITED
December 1954

"Come on, Biddy, we'll have a grand time. Ye need to go out and have fun, ye've been moping about here for too long. Ah go on, Bridget…"

I laughed, and threw a dirty dishrag at Una who was carrying a pile of plates towards the sink. My hands were plunged up to the elbows in greasy hot water as I wiped and scrubbed dirty cutlery for the diners in the restaurant of Owen & Owen department store in Coventry.

After three unhappy years in Manchester, I moved to Coventry in February 1954, at the age of 25, hoping for a fresh start. I'd been back to the infirmary as an inpatient after another failed suicide attempt and had spent many months there undergoing ECT again and finally being discharged with prescriptions for anti-depressants and sleeping tablets. It was the last time I tried to kill myself, and again, it was the sadness I felt at losing my child, and my loved ones, that drove me back into that terrible place where pills and a bottle of gin offered a blessed escape from my failed life.

The second time I was admitted, after one of my neighbours found me slumped on my bed in my room, I was told I was lucky to be alive. I didn't feel lucky, even though things had improved a little. I'd found work after leaving the infirmary following my first suicide attempt. Strangely, I'd found the position – cleaning a nearby pub – enjoyable. The landlord had been kindly, and if he thought I'd done a good job he'd give me a couple of free beers and would sit to chat with me in a friendly way. That companionship gave me some comfort, but against the background of the demons I started to realise had followed me from Ireland, it was a drop of kindness in a vast, cruel ocean.

Now I had some distance from Roscrea and Templemore, my sadness had turned to anger. Such a deep rage, I felt hollowed out by it. My moods swung between laughter and jollity, and wild, uncontrollable anger. Eventually, I shouted at the customers in the pub one too many times and I was dismissed, leaving me anchorless again. It was then my drinking took off. This time I was using the bottle to dampen down my fury rather than comfort my sorrow. I was angry at the nuns in Roscrea for their lies, for taking my son. I felt like they'd punished me for my perceived crime of having a child out of wedlock. I felt furious that the priest in Templemore had ignored the truth, that I was a victim of rape, which was a mortal sin against me. I hated the priest, I hated the nuns, I hated Robert above all. I could picture his face, screwed up as he entered me roughly, taking my virginity from me in a vicious act of hatred and control. I hated the Moral Welfare Officer for leaving me at the Sean Ross Abbey, for putting me into the hands of those nuns, for letting them take my Kieran away from me. I even hated Bill for running away when he should've come for me and taken me with him.

But most of all, I hated myself. Even then, I could see how powerless I was against the forces that controlled me, and it sickened me. So I drank and drank, anything to take away the burning within me. I started to become notorious in the pubs nearby. When I entered, making my way straight to the bar, I saw nods and winks. Well, I didn't care. I had a fury in my head that wouldn't abate and I didn't know another way to remove it, even for just a few hours.

Back in the asylum, I was subjected to more of their 'treatments'. I submitted to everything, though fits of anger came and went and it seemed to make little difference. Eventually I was prescribed the anti-depressants that were only given to patients in mental hospitals at the time. Gradually I felt brighter, my moods calmed and the doctors declared I was fit to be released. Clutching my medication, which also included sleeping tablets, I left, vowing to myself that however bad it got, I would never go back there. Hope seemed to enter the cracks inside me like light through a curtain.

I was feeling as if I could start my life again. I'd found myself another job in the department store kitchen, and though the pay wasn't wonderful, I'd felt proud of myself for the first time. I was finally earning a regular wage and looking forward to getting up each morning. I felt like I'd rejoined the human race!

Part of my happiness in my new job was the fact I'd made a good friend in Una. We hit it off on the first day after one of the managers, a spinster in her 50s who liked nothing better than to complain incessantly about us younger women, pulled me up on my uniform. I'd hurried into work, nervous, and sporting a dull headache from the tipple I'd had the night before to calm my nerves. I seemed to make every mistake possible. My uniform was creased. My hair wasn't tied back as it should be. And I was wearing lipstick! All of these transgressions were brought swiftly to my attention.

"Miss Larkin, if you will insist on looking scruffy then we cannot accommodate you here," declared Miss Smith in front of the entire kitchen staff.

I looked down at my shoes. My stockings were already wrinkled.

"If you will not comport yourself with the required level of dignity, then your place will be filled by someone who can. Girls are queuing up to work here." She sniffed, arching her brows and pursing her thin lips. Her collars were starched, her uniform impeccable.

"Sorry Miss Smith. It won't happen again, I promise," I muttered miserably, feeling like I'd already failed in my duties and it was only the first day.

"Don't ye go worryin' about her Bridget. She's a right old dragon, an absolute bitch. Stick with me and ye'll be alright." The pretty blonde girl had sidled up to me the moment Miss Smith had left the room. "My name's Una," she smiled.

"And ye can call me Biddy," I replied, grateful for her kind words.

"But you're Irish as well. Where are ye from, Una?"

"I'm from Tipperary," she answered, handing me a broom to sweep up the vegetable peelings.

"Jaysus, so am I!" I cried, turning to Una, my face flushed with surprise and happiness. "But, why are ye here, Una? It's so far from home…" I didn't know if it was too soon to ask questions but I desperately wanted to hear more about the country of my birth, and to meet someone who was from the same part of Ireland felt like a small miracle, one that instantly soothed the continual ache of homesickness, a feeling that never really left me despite my unhappy memories of the place.

Una was a refugee of sorts, too, adrift from her homeland just like me. I could sense that she felt the same way, too.

"Ach well ye see, Biddy, I got myself into trouble. I don't like talking about it… I fell for a local lad and he promised to wed me but it didn't work out that way. When he knew I was havin' his baby, things changed. His mother didn't like me. Thought I wasn't good enough for her son. I begged him not to leave me, to bring up our child together, but it didn't work." Una shrugged. "Anyway, I found myself at Roscrea…" At that point her voice trailed off and her face changed.

I leapt over to Una and snatched up her hands. "Ye went to Roscrea, to the abbey home? I was practically shaking her hands. "I was there too. I had a littl' boy called Kieran. He was the most gorgeous bonny littl' thing… I had to leave him. They sent me away, too much scandal."

I felt a sudden lump in my throat. I dropped Una's hands as if they scalded me.

"Oh Biddy. They did the same to me,' said Una. "I try to think that at least they let me keep her for three years, at least I got that time with my littl' girl even if it made the parting with her all the harder. She was called Aileen. I don't know what *they* called her.

"An American family came over on an aeroplane and took her. I know she will have a better life there, better than I could ever give her and I try to be grateful for that, so I do. Sometimes I can't even remember what she looks like."

A tear slid down my face. "You had three years, that's something. I had six days with Kieran – six days. I wonder who is holding him, soothing him at night, feeding him and changing his nappies. I can't stop thinking of him." My voice croaked with the pain that simply never went away.

"And I bet that bitch Sister Hildegarde is still there, wreaking her revenge on the female sex. 'Ye'll all go to hell, ye're all sinners!'" rasped Una, copying the nun's voice so completely that I could almost see her standing in front of me.

I couldn't help smiling at that and wiped my face with a grubby sleeve. "Well, we'd better watch out for each other. I can't believe ye've been through the same as me. Nobody else could ever understand how it feels, could they?"

Una nodded and touched my arm with a gentle show of solidarity.

"Get back to work! You're not being paid to gossip!" came Miss Smith's voice and we both hurried back to our tasks, me sweeping the broom while Una carried rubbish out to the bins.

Here we were again, working together as we'd made sure our shifts coincided, and Una was suggesting a night out. We'd already had a few jaunts out. Our wages meant this was a rare luxury, but I was also constrained by the money I spent on my nightly drinks. I was still seeking solace in alcohol.

Inside, I felt like my heart was irretrievably broken by the loss of my son, and the only real comfort I knew in the dark lonely hours of the night came from the bottle. I knew it could be a slippery slope into madness, and each evening I vowed to myself that it was the last time I'd medicate myself with drink. But every evening, as the darkness fell, I was beset by my memories; of my stepfather's suicide, of my brother's attack, of the beloved child I bore – and was parted from. My mood would sink lower, fuelled by the drink but also soothed by it. The shock and trauma I'd experienced faded away for a few blissful hours, until I woke up with a headache, a burning thirst and all the good intentions I could summon.

Each night back in my bedsit near Dudley Lodge, those good intentions dissolved into my cups of sherry or gin, and there seemed little I could do to change things. I knew that by suggesting a night out, Una was trying to help me. I'm sure she suspected that my drinking was not fully under my control, and she mentioned a few times that I smelled of booze, but she always dismissed it with a light-hearted laugh, probably to spare my feelings.

"Biddy, ye need a good night out. We can have a laugh, and you never know, we may even find ourselves a good catch!"

I giggled at that.

"Alright. I'm starting to see that if I don't agree, then I'll never hear the end of it!"

"You're absolutely right, Biddy. I shall keep on at ye until you agree. I'm relentless as ye know!" Una chuckled, handing me a batch of dirty plates.

"Ach, this job never gets nicer, does it?" I sighed, up to my arms in the suds. My hands were still badly chapped from my work at the laundry and the water made them sting.

"I need a new frock though, I'm not goin' anywhere without a new dress," I bantered.

"Sounds good to me! Well I'll get the tickets, we'll go to the Christmas dance at that Irish bar in Hurst Street. We'll have a proper night out in Birmingham, and if that doesn't cheer ye up, Biddy, nothing will."

As it turned out, that night in Birmingham was beyond anything I could have dreamed of. I was queuing at the bar to buy myself and Una a drink when I heard someone behind me say, "Well now, let me treat ye." I spun round, thinking I was going mad to hear that voice. That same voice that had stopped me in my tracks the first time I heard it at the funfair. I wasn't mad. There he was, large as life, leaning over the counter.

"It can't be you Biddy, my own true sweetheart? I never thought I'd see you again." Bill's kind face peered into my eyes.

It was the man I fell in love with, the face I had dreamed about seeing again and by some miracle of God, he was here, in Birmingham. I could hardly believe my eyes.

"It's you," I breathed.

While I stood there, open mouthed, probably looking a proper fool, he was as cool as a cucumber. Fixing his twinkling eyes on my gobsmacked face, he looked for all the world as though he expected to see me.

"And don't ye look beautiful in your green dress. Green suits you, Biddy. Jaysus I've missed ye."

I finally untwisted my tongue. "Bill, it can't be you, it can't. How come you're here? What happened in Templemore? Why did ye leave me?" My questions came tumbling out as an unstoppable force.

Bill stopped smiling and he suddenly lost his confident twinkle. He grabbed my arm and steered me towards a dark corner.

"This way... I can't speak here."

I followed him, not caring about the drinks, or even about poor Una, sat all by herself at one of the tables. In that moment I cared only for Bill, and the sight of him had sent me into an almost trance-like state. How could this be happening? Was I dreaming? Was this real?

The brush of his mouth against my ear told me it was.

"Biddy. I'm so sorry. I let ye down." He paused for a second and I sat silently, holding my breath, willing him to put everything right. "Your brother came round that night," he continued. "He told me he'd kill me if I stayed in Ireland. I truly believe he would have, Biddy. Ach, I know I should've been braver. I should've stayed for ye, or taken ye with me, but..."

"He's a scary man," I finished for him. I knew that well

enough, but looking at Bill I felt a complicated twist in my stomach. Of course Robert was frightening to me, a young woman, but to a strapping lad who worked on a farm? A man like Bill should never have backed down in front of my brother, and I felt the betrayal keenly still. If he had really loved me, surely he would have fought for me. Reluctant as I was to admit this, Bill could read my thoughts, just as he always could, as if we were the same person split in two.

"I let you down Biddy, I know that, and I don't suppose ye'll ever forgive me. But I meant it when I said I loved you."

I believed him. One look at his open, contrite face told me he was being truthful. I could feel that knot of doubt melting away.

"God, Biddy, ye look gorgeous," he said. "That colour. It's the first time I've seen ye wear green, it makes your skin sparkle." Bill looked as handsome and sweet as I remembered. He pulled his hands through his blond hair, his features dark in the bar's smoky interior. My heart swooped to my stomach and I knew I was his, body and soul. I knew that whatever happened, whatever had gone before, I wanted to be with Bill.

"Do ye forgive me, Biddy? I couldn't live with myself if ye didn't."

I gazed up into his blue eyes and nodded. I couldn't help myself: all my doubts, my anger, my pain just fell away. There was nothing but me and him.

"Of course I do, Bill. I love ye as much today as I ever did. I wish you'd taken me with ye though, I wanted ye to. I missed ye so much."

My stomach flipped over as I felt, rather than saw, Bill lean in towards me to plant a tender kiss on my waiting lips. "I never stopped loving you Biddy," he whispered tenderly.

Someone started playing the piano, one of those maudlin

Irish lilts about green lands and lost love. Bill put his hand in the curve of my waist and drew me to him. My legs felt like jelly underneath me as we swayed gently together to the music, our eyes locked. Then a voice yelled across to the pianist, "Jaysus Sean, could you cheer things up a bit? You'll have us all weepin' into our Guinness! Play something a bit lively would ya?"

Bill suddenly shouted, "Play *It's a Long Way to Tipperary*." Sean the pianist grinned, and struck up the first chords. Soon the whole pub seemed to be singing 'our song', as Bill pulled me into the centre of the area being used as a dance floor. His arms curled round me and he held me close as he sang his own version to me, his breath causing me to shiver and swoon with the pleasure of it. "It's a long way to Tipperary, it's a long way to go. It's a long way to Tipperary, to the sweetest girl I know. Hello Tipperary Mary, how I love you so, Now I've found my Tipperary Mary, I will never let her go!"

I saw, briefly, Una's face as he danced me round. She looked awe-struck. She was standing up, her mouth wide open, agog with the spectacle of her best friend being twirled round the floor by the most handsome man in the bar.

At the end of the song, Bill cheered, and I laughed with the first real happiness I'd experienced since he'd left.

Panting with exhilaration and exertion, we arrived back at the table where Una was now sitting.

"This is Bill," I said, and he leaned over to shake her hand in a rather sweetly formal manner.

"Oh… Bill…" replied Una, her eyes widening and, for once, stuck for something to say.

I laughed at the sight of her, unable to hide her knowledge of the man who had stolen my heart so completely.

Another song struck up. "Again!" Bill cried and swung me on

to the impromptu dancefloor, where we stayed for the rest of the evening, reeling and swirling among the merry throng until we were breathless. Eventually, we rejoined Una at the table where she was laughingly waving off Bill's hopeful pal Pete.

"We can't compete with those lovebirds," she said, as Bill held me close and nuzzled into my hair.

"Let's get some air," Bill whispered. I nodded, feeling a little faint with the heat and the revelry and my own giddy excitement.

We stepped outside. It was a bitter cold night. Bill took off his coat and draped it round my shoulders. I staggered a little with the effects of the beer we had been drinking.

I realised he had brought me into a small alley that ran off the main drag of bars and late-night drinking spots.

'Oh Biddy, God I've missed ye. I thought I'd never see ye again."

Before I could say anything his mouth closed over mine, his hands tracing the contours of my face, pulling back my hair and kissing me until I couldn't breathe.

I brought my hands up to hold his, to feel his skin against mine. It was then I felt it – the hard band of metal that circled his ring finger. I stopped breathing. How could this be true? He brought his hand up to brush back my wayward hair again, and that's when I saw the glint of gold. There was no mistaking it. A wedding ring. Men rarely wore wedding rings then, so it was doubly shocking to see one on his hand. I hadn't noticed it because it never occurred to me for a second that he might be wearing one. Why would it, after the way he had been loving me all night?

I pushed him back.

"What is it, Biddy, ye don't know how I've thought about

this," Bill murmured, his breath hot on my neck as he drew me back towards him.

"You're married." It was a statement not a question.

Stumbling back, away from him, I grabbed the wall for support.

We just looked at one another in silence, the seconds stretching like hours. "Ye don't have to say anything. I understand." I said finally. I didn't understand. I didn't understand how this could be happening.

Bill looked at me. His face crumpled.

"But, Biddy..." he started to say, touching his ring with his left hand, almost to pull it off his finger. I turned away, walked back up the alley, into the bar to find Una, my heart as cold as the ice that glistened across the cobbles.

CHAPTER 14

SECRET ENCOUNTERS
August 1955

"It isn't much, but it's ours for the whole weekend." Bill opened the door to our small room in the guesthouse in Burnham-on-Sea. He'd whisked me away from Birmingham for this precious time together in Somerset.

"It's lovely! I love it!" I exclaimed, peering round at the chintzy peach curtains, the fussy doilies on the washstand and, most wonderful of all, our own double bed! "Come here," I said and winked, which made Bill laugh. He sidled over to me and kissed me squarely on the mouth. I couldn't get enough of him, his smell, his embrace, his hard body against mine.

Bill now worked in a metal factory in Birmingham, a rough job that required enormous physical power to work the machinery. His arms rippled with muscles and every time I felt them round me, my knees turned to jelly.

I laughed raucously as he whispered to me what he wanted to do next, and shoved him away playfully.

"Let's go and see the sea first, we can do all of that later," I laughed, grabbing my cardie as there was a breeze despite the summer sunshine. Bill pretended to sulk, pouting like a child, but he grabbed his flat cap and we walked out, arm-in-arm and looking for all the world like a respectably married couple.

We strolled out of the guesthouse down a few quiet streets

until we found the beach, which stretched as far as the eye could see.

"We're free!!!" I exclaimed, throwing off my shoes and running onto the sand, followed by Bill in hot pursuit. I didn't care that there were families sitting on deckchairs, their children making sandcastles, as I cried: 'Wheeeeee, we're freeeeee."

"You're mad, Biddy Larkin, my own Tipperary Mary! Totally mad!" shouted Bill as he chased me, catching me easily and wrestling me to the ground.

We were, by now, a little way from the families, out of earshot if not sight, and Bill held me down by my wrists and lay on top of me, careful not to crush me. His face hovered inches from mine, and I felt the familiar pull of my senses, the eagerness within me to be with him. Call me wanton. Call me a loose woman. I didn't care. My love for Bill overrode everything – even the fact that he had a wife.

My face must've changed as Bill suddenly looked puzzled. He pulled away, lying next to me on the beach.

"What is it, Biddy?"

I sighed.

"No matter how far away we come, I can never forget that ye have a wife, Bill, and a baby son. Sometimes I look at myself in the mirror and I hate myself for what we're doin' yet I can't seem to stop."

There was silence for a moment, except for an insistent fly buzzing around our heads.

Bill took a long breath.

"We've been over this, darling. I don't love her, I never did. She fell pregnant shortly after we met and she said it was mine. What could I do? I couldn't leave her could I now?"

I had told Bill everything over the months since we found

each other again. Even though I'd walked away from him that night we met again, I found myself back in that bar the following week. I hadn't been able to get Bill out of my mind. I remembered his smell, the feel of his hand on me, his eyes staring intently in mine. I wrestled with my conscience, even turned to God to help me but I knew I was beyond help. When it came to Bill I was helpless to resist. I'd had so little love and affection in my life.

So it was with a feeling of inevitability that I found myself back at the same bar, standing at the counter and looking around the room with a feeling of excitement and fear. Bill was there, as I knew he would be, and without a word he walked over to me, embraced me and took me back to my lodgings. We barely spoke on the way there. We'd crept in. I knew I'd be kicked out if I was spotted entertaining a man in my room but I was beyond sense or reason. The first night we'd just talked and that's when I told him about my rape at the hands of my brother, the subsequent child and his adoption to America from the Roscrea home for mothers and babies. He'd listened intently. When I finished I turned to him and his eyes were filled with tears. "I should've been there to protect ye, Biddy, I should've been there." He kept saying it over and over again until it was me who shushed him, who held him close. No-one had ever cared for me before, not properly. The only other person I'd ever truly loved – and felt loved by – was my sister Philomena, and she was lost to me now. It went without saying that I had loved my son, and always would, but that was more of a pain that ripped at me, never letting go of me, always threatening to drag me down into a pit of my own suffering. I wasn't used to someone loving me enough to cry for me. It moved me sincerely when Bill showed such remorse for leaving me.

We'd seen each other every week since then, sometimes daily. I'd fallen head over heels in love with him again, even though the sight of that ring always gave me such turmoil. Bill told me he'd wed the girl after getting her in trouble, and it was an unhappy union. He implored me to believe him and I did because I wanted to, needed to. When he'd asked me to spend a weekend with him by the seaside I didn't hesitate to say yes.

"I'm going to leave her, Biddy. I love you, my Tipperary Mary, just you, but I can't do it yet. Anyway she's gone back to Ireland. She struggled with the baby, and me working long hours, so she went home to her family. She's out of my life now, Biddy, ye have to believe me."

I turned round to him, kissing him softly. "Of course I believe ye, Bill. I just wish things weren't like this, that we could be free to marry and not hurt anyone in the process." There was nothing he could say to that.

Things weren't as clear as Bill made out, though. Many times over the months since we'd been reunited, I'd asked Bill if I could see his lodgings, but he always refused, saying he shared them and it wouldn't be right to bring me there. There was sense in what he said. As an unmarried woman it was frowned upon to meet with a married man at his home, but something inside me told me it was more than that. After all, I only had Bill's word that his wife and child had left him. Bill said time and time again that he only loved me and that he had only been doing the 'decent' thing by marrying her, yet he refused to show me where he was living.

Every time we met, he'd come to my lodgings, or my workplace, and we'd go back to mine. And I never knew her name. Bill refused to tell me, saying he didn't want to speak of her, she was nothing compared to me, but it struck me as odd. Did he think I'd try to find her? Meet her, even? Did he think I'd try to tell her about our affair, the secret encounters we'd contrived over the past months? I pushed all my doubts out of sight but try as I might, I couldn't make them go away entirely.

"But Bill, what are ye goin' to do about her? We can't go on lying," I said on that August day at the beach.

"I promise I'll tell her about ye soon, and then you and I will be free to wed. I promise ye Biddy."

I smiled, my heart beating a little faster. He looked so sincere. His blue eyes bore into mine, and so I nodded my response, though my stomach tightened. I knew I was smitten, but at the back of my mind was the memory of him leaving me with Robert. Somehow that memory never faded, however much I willed it away. And, of course, he was betraying his wedding vows. Even now, looking back into his startlingly blue eyes there was a whisper inside saying 'watch out', 'beware', and yet I couldn't stop myself. For once, I was so happy. "Alright, that's settled. Now let's get some fish and chips, then it's back to our room. I can't wait any longer for ye Biddy." I smiled a delicious smile, the look of a woman well-loved, with a man who wanted her, body and soul. 'Or perhaps we could have our supper later..." I replied, arching an eyebrow.

With that, Bill whooped, grabbed my hand and pelted along the shore until we arrived back at our room, breathless with running and ignited passion. As soon as the door was locked, he pulled the curtains shut and threw off his shoes. He came over to me and said: "Turn around."

I obeyed without thinking, my eyes closing in anticipation of the pleasure that was to follow. Slowly, he undid my dress, pulled off my slip and stockings and laid me on the bed. He undressed himself. I stared up at him, the only man I had ever loved, and all thoughts of telling his wife disappeared in the melting together of my body and his.

Lying in Bill's arms on the bed, the covers strewn across the floor as a result of our love-making, my head on his smooth chest, I felt completely content.

After a while, I rolled away from him. "Let's go and get a little glass of something, Bill," I said. I had started feeling an itch for a drink every afternoon around the same time.

Bill lifted his head up and stared at me intently.

"Biddy, I know ye like a drink, but don't ye think ye should ease off a little? We've hours yet before the pubs shut."

"I like a drink, there's no crime in that is there?" I sniffed, offended at the concern in his voice, yet he was only saying what others had already said to me, including my pal Una.

I'd been in trouble with the police on a couple of occasions during nights out with my friend: after too many gins washed down with beer, I would be in hot water for cursing and screeching, and generally acting in a disorderly fashion. The next day I'd always feel horrified when Una recounted what I'd done. "I'm worried about ye," she'd say, and I'd shrug it off with, "Well don't be worried. I'm fine. I just like to enjoy myself, that's all. Don't ye go telling me what I can and can't do, Una, I'm alright, really." Una would nod, looking unconvinced but accepting I was in charge of my own life finally, and what I did with it.

Despite my insistence, I knew I drank too much, but I hated it being pointed out, after all, I had few other comforts – apart from Bill – in my life. In fact, it was the lonely nights when I couldn't see my sweetheart that I turned increasingly to the bottle. Alone and missing him, I'd buy two bottles of beer on my way home from a shift in the kitchens, to supplement the ever-decreasing bottles of gin I had started stashing away under my bed. I knew that things were starting to get out of control, but as the night darkened my sorrow at being parted from Bill deepened, and the questions whispered in the back of my mind, said 'Will it always be like this?' 'Will he really leave his wife?' and 'Will he ever be mine, body and soul?'. It was much easier to drink myself into oblivion rather than face things I didn't want to see.

"Alright, I'll wait," I grumbled, putting my thirst for a drink on hold. "That's my girl, now let's see if we can find a way to pass the time..." We'd only just made love. Bill's passion for me was unquenchable, as was mine for him, and his desire for me overrode all my niggling doubts about him. He'd let me down badly in the past, he was cheating on his wife, but he could not disguise his need for me, his body responding to me, and it gave me hope for the future. Bill slid his leg over me and pulled me into his embrace. I sighed the soft sigh of a happy woman as the ecstasy of his touch overwhelmed me.

The next morning, I woke early to the sound of seagulls. I lay revelling in the feeling of being close to Bill as his breathing gradually surfaced as if from a deep well, and his eyes fluttered open.

"I was dreaming of ye. Come here and show me you're not just a fabrication of my mind," he murmured, grinning.

I kissed him long and hard and felt his body stir beneath the sheets. We made love again, before each of us, wrapped in our robes, tiptoed out of the room to use the bathroom and have a brisk, cold wash. When we'd checked in to the guest house, Bill had handed me a thin, metal band, which just about fitted on my wedding finger.

'Ye'll need this or they won't let us stay," he'd whispered. "We're Mr and Mrs Ryan from Coventry, if anyone asks," he winked.

I blushed.

I looked down at the cheap ring on my finger and felt a surge of joy. I remembered the plastic one that he had given me at the funfair all those years ago – it had been as precious to me as if it were made of solid gold. Perhaps one day, I would wear a real wedding ring given to me by Bill. The thought filled me with nervous excitement.

I made sure I was wearing the ring as we sauntered down to the poky front room for breakfast. Tea and toast were set out on the small table by the window. The elderly, plump matriarch who ran the establishment, looked us up and down – causing me to blush deeply – before asking: "Full English is it? For both of you? Or should I say Full Irish?"

I coughed, stifling my giggles.

Bill answered smoothly.

'That would be grand, thank ye."

"So you are Irish, are you?"

As we knew, Irish weren't always welcome. England and Ireland had a long history of trouble, with the Fenians, or Fenian Brotherhood as they had been properly known, fighting at the end of the last century to overturn British rule in Southern Ireland. We now had independence, which had bred a mutual suspicion between the English and Irish, and there were still bars and lodgings that had signs up saying 'No Irish' even in 1955.

"Ach, yes, but we left there years ago. We haven't been back since," said Bill conversationally, and the woman soon moved away, distracted by another resident.

"Phew, that was close, I thought she was going to kick us out!" joked Bill, though I knew we were skating on thin ice and if she realised we weren't married I shuddered to think of the hulla-baloo it would cause.

I settled back to munch on my toast, the bright sunlight pouring in through the window. I had never felt happier, except when holding little Kieran in my arms, though of course that was tinged with sadness as well. I now had the same sense of being on borrowed time. However much I enjoyed playing Bill's 'wife', I knew that our precious time was nearly up. We were heading back to Coventry that day, and I would become Bill's mistress again, a position I knew in my heart was wrong. After breakfast we wandered back to the seaside and went for a paddle. I stood at the water's edge, my toes sinking in to the sand, feeling the sun on my face. My heart was light, carefree, yet we only had a few short hours before boarding the train that would take us back to the Midlands.

"Y'know I love ye, Biddy." Bill gripped my hand tightly and led me further into the water.

'I love ye too, Bill, ye know I do," I smiled back at him. Then, knee-deep in the cool, refreshing sea, we kissed passionately as if we were entirely alone there. I knew we would be raising yet more eyebrows on the beach, but we hoped people would assume we were newlyweds on our honeymoon. It was plausible enough!

Just then a wave rolled in and knocked us both off our balance. I stumbled, clutching at Bill as we both fell, splash, into the water.

"Jaysus, Holy Mother of God!" Bill swore, as he sprung up and helped me to my feet. My skirt was soaking but I didn't care. The sun would dry us off, so we headed back to the shore and sat on the warm sand, hand-in-hand, waiting for the sun to do its work, chatting idly about the future; where we would live, how many babies we would have. The thought of holding Bill's child in my arms was a blissful one. We chose names for our imaginary children, and decided we would settle in Somerset where no-one would bother us, and no-one would know our pasts. Bill said his fantasy was for me to carry our child, a little Bill or Biddy all of our own. I snuggled into his arms, listening to the seagulls shriek and the waves move against the shore. Bill kissed the top of my head and gave a long sigh. He didn't need to tell me why. I knew he was feeling the same wistful, yearning as me. If only life could be simple. If only Bill's wife could magically disappear and leave us to our love. If only we really could have children together and set up home. I truly believed that, for both of us, that dream gave us real happiness.

Later, we fetched our suitcase from the room, said a swift goodbye to the owner so as not to raise any more questions, and headed to the coach station to catch the bus that would take us to the train station.

As we walked, I felt my creeping loneliness hovering in the back of my mind. I didn't want our trip to end. I couldn't bear the thought of kissing Bill goodbye at Birmingham New Street, and walking off in our separate directions.

"Promise me we'll be married," I said, stopping Bill and standing in front of him.

He looked away, not speaking.

"Ye know I love ye, Biddy, ye know it," was all he said.

"But I didn't ask ye that, Bill," I replied softly. Looking back I realise that this was the moment my dreams vanished, popped like a colourful balloon. In that split second, I saw his weakness, how society and the church wrapped around him and kept me out. He turned back to me and with his easy smile said: 'Of course I will. I promise beloved," and he kissed me again. The lightest touch on my lips that left them tingling. We would spend the rest of our lives together, and nothing, or no-one would stop us. That was our fantasy but somewhere, deep down, I knew it could never become reality.

I didn't go straight home. I went to church, sliding round the large wooden doors, to light candles. One for Kieran, one for Philomena, one for Bill, and the last for Bill's wife, whoever she was. I knew that either God had forsaken me, or I Him. I rarely attended Mass now, feeling too guilty about my shameful secret. I was having an affair with a married man, which was forbidden by God, but I knew in my heart I couldn't stop seeing him. Even the risk of eternal damnation wouldn't stop me. I was a woman in love. A woman of 26 now and desperate for a family of my own at last, and this time I was determined I would have a child with my beloved.

CHAPTER 15

JUST A DREAM...
November 1955 to May 1956

"A baby – no. Come on Biddy, you're having me on," spluttered Bill. His face had turned pink, his voice went up a few pitches. I sat, watching him, holding my still-flat stomach, though it wouldn't be for much longer.

"Yes, Bill, a baby, we've made a baby, don't ye see? I couldn't be happier, truly I couldn't. We've made our very own little Bill or Biddy to love forever, just as we dreamed of. It's a special day, so it is. I wasn't sure at first, so I wanted to wait until I was certain before I told you. You're goin' to be a daddy." I could feel my face alight with joy. A baby of our own! Bill had no choice now – he would have to leave her and marry me.

Bill looked at me for a long moment, and I saw the struggle within him. I snatched hold of his hands. "Just think, Bill, a baby, our baby... Can ye imagine anything more wonderful?"

Bill dropped my hands, turned away and drew them through his oiled hair.

"But Biddy, my Biddy. I'm already a daddy..."

I stared at him, thinking I'd misheard.

"Yes, my darlin', I know, but we talked about the children we wanted so often. D'ye remember? We even gave them names, we wanted our own babies so badly." I gripped Bill's hands, but instead of turning to me and acknowledging our shared wishes, he moved backwards, taking back his hands.

"Bill?"

"I'm sorry, Biddy. I can't do this. You of all people should know that. I'm already a daddy. I have a wife and a child. Jaysus, what have I done?"

He sat abruptly on my bed and put his head between his hands.

"Bill, come on Bill. This isn't you talking. We wanted a baby, well here it is, our child, Bill, think of that."

"I am thinking, Biddy, one of us has to!" Bill's voice was harsher than I expected and I recoiled.

My heart froze in my chest as I saw the panicked look settle on his face. This wasn't what I'd expected, hoped for. This wasn't our moment of happiness as I'd imagined it to be. I felt confused, the seeds of disappointment had already been sown inside me, yet I knew Bill was a good man. I knew he wouldn't let me down, didn't I..? Didn't I?

Suddenly I felt anger rear up inside me. I couldn't stop my outburst: "Ye have no choice, ye have to leave her and marry me. Bill, I of all people know ye have another family. But I'm not responsible for their wellbeing. It's been your choice to be with me. You're the one who has said a thousand times that ye wish you'd never married her. Jaysus I don't even know your wife's name!?"

I stopped when I saw Bill's face blanche. This was clearly a shock for him.

I realised I'd better tread more lightly. I softened my tone and continued.

"We're your family now. Me and this baby that we both made. I love ye Bill, ye know I love ye with my heart and soul, and this baby is a gift from God, don't ye see that?

"Bill, darlin', just tell me that you're goin' to write to her and tell her it's over at last. That's all ye need to do. We can say you've been separated for years and so it won't be difficult getting a divorce. I knew a girl in Templemore who did just that – "

Before I could continue, Bill cut me off. His voice was raised, the anguish clear on his face: "Yes, Bridget," he said, emphasising my real name, the one he never used, "and I bet no-one ever spoke to her or her new husband again. I bet she couldn't hold her head high. I bet that after the gossiping, and the spite, she was left to herself. I bet she was called 'whore' and spat on in the street. The priests, they preach God's love from the pulpit but did ye ever see it in action, Biddy? Did ye see the milk of human kindness running through the town?"

I stared back at him, shifting uncomfortably as I sat next to him on the bed. Bill might be exaggerating, but he wasn't far wrong. I knew women in Ireland were second-class citizens and could so easily become a social outcast. The girl I knew had suffered, and in the end she and her baby had left the area to start a new life away from family, friends and community. But I didn't care about any of that. They could all go to hell. No-one in England knew my family, and if they did, I was already dead to them. So why was Bill looking so flustered, so unhappy?

"No, divorce is not an option, Biddy, ye know that. It's a sin, and whatever I think of the priests, I don't want to be mired in sin."

"Then our baby is a sin, then our love is a feckin' sin!" My voice rose. I knew I had to calm down, for the baby's sake, but I couldn't. "How could ye say that?" I sobbed. "I've spent the last years missing ye, then waiting, never knowin' when I'd see ye next. If ye want cruelty, then look in the mirror!" I was panting now, overcome with feelings of hurt and fear. This wasn't going the way I thought it would at all.

"Jaysus feckin' Christ! I didn't expect this," ranted Bill, pausing every so often to lean his head against the peeling wallpaper.

"But ye must've known there was a risk of this happening," I said, knowing I hadn't been worried when Bill didn't hold back during our lovemaking. "Ye never mentioned it before so I assumed ye wanted it as much as I did. But even that is irrelevant. Our baby is here, inside me, and we just have to get on with it. Ye've no choice. Ye have to leave her."

It seemed so obvious to me. I had fallen pregnant with my lover's child. We loved one another, always had, and wanted to be together. There must be no more delays. It was time he did the right thing by me, and left the woman he professed not to love to become my husband.

"Jaysus Christ... Jaysus..." Bill now paced up and down the narrow strip of floor between my makeshift bed and the window, which looked out onto rows of other grey terraces.

"Stop it! Just stop. I can't see what's so terribly wrong, Bill?" It was just a lover's tiff surely, sparked by the shock of my news. Bill would soon stop this, I told myself, sink onto his knees and kiss my hands in apology. I smiled up at him as I reminded myself why we were having this fight.

Even though it was early days, I was only just past the three-month mark, I swore I could sense this new life growing bigger each second of each day inside me. He would see the light any second, and we'd rejoice about the baby. Surely he would.

Instead, Bill turned to me, his face like marble, his eyes glinting in the flickering evening light. "Don't ye see, Biddy, this changes everything. I'm sorry, I truly am. I need to take it in, get my head straight."

I blinked. Bill had told me every time we met that he loved me and wanted nothing more than to leave his wife and be with me. He'd told me we were soulmates, destined to be together. So why then was he behaving like a terrified child?

"Bill, sweetheart, I don't understand. I thought ye loved me.' My voice was small in that overcrowded room. My lodgings consisted of a single iron bed, a small stove and a single cupboard. I had very few possessions; a wooden rosary, my prayer book, some clothing and a few books, which were tattered and old. I always had a good supply of gin or sherry kept indoors, but even that had been left untouched with the rising tide of morning sickness – which seemed to last all day.

"Course I do, course I do. Now, don't ye go frettin'," soothed Bill, though his eyes wouldn't meet mine.

I heard myself plead: "But you said ye loved me, you'd leave your wife for me – that's what ye said." I repeated it as if it would somehow make sense, as if it would somehow make him be true to his word.

My beloved's silence told me everything I needed to know. There were no joyful kisses, no delight at my news. Bill seemed to be shrinking away from me, vanishing in front of my eyes. He wouldn't even look at me. I tried to reach for his hand to place on my tummy, but he snatched it away as fast as a snake, grabbing for the door handle.

With a jolt, I felt nauseous but it wasn't the baby this time. In that moment, I saw all my romantic dreams of Bill proposing to me, singing to our child in my belly, placing his child in his arms, getting married, all of it crumbled into nothingness.

I saw then what I should have known all along; that he'd never had any intention of leaving her. I was a distraction, an affair that was in the process of ending.

"Please Bill, don't do this to me," I stammered, standing up. But before I could say another word, my sweetheart was by the door, guilt written over his face.

"I'm sorry, Biddy, I'm sorry." And with that, he turned tail and left. I stared after him, my world collapsing around me. Before I could think, before I could break down into sobs, I reached for the bottle of sherry that stood next to the stove. With a shaking hand I poured out a cupful, brought it to my lips and without a moment's hesitation, drank it down in one go. It was then that emotion spilled from me. I sank to my knees, crying out and shaking. Bill had gone – and something inside me knew it was for good this time. But I wasn't ready to let him go. Sometimes all you have is hope, even if reality makes a mockery of it.

Several days later, as I woke up and yawned, stretching out my arms, I felt my stomach jolt. I lurched out of bed and threw up in the kitchen bucket, retching the contents of my stomach, feeling for a rag to wipe my mouth with. Not the best start to my birthday.

My morning sickness had kicked in again, not helped by my nightly cups of sherry, though I was just starting my second trimester. Since the day Bill had left I'd carried on, going to work, seeing Una and doing my chores, but all the while I felt like I was living in a bubble of my misery, one that separated me from the rest of the world. I hated myself for being so foolish, so taken in by his easy charm and empty flattery. I had known it was wrong to be seeing a married man but I didn't care and here was my punishment. Left alone, pregnant, uncertain what the future held. What was even worse, I sometimes still allowed myself to hope that he'd come round. He may be able to turn his back on me a second time, but his own baby? Then the despair would kick in and I would hit the bottle and cry myself to sleep. The baby was the thing that kept me going, this tiny little life inside me, depending on me. And I would not let this baby down, like I had Kieran.

After I'd finished being sick and rinsed out the bowl in the bathroom, I sat back on my bed, my legs feeling wobbly. It was a Friday, and so I had to be at work in an hour, despite how rough I felt. I dressed slowly, buttoning up my skirt and smoothing down my wrinkled blouse. I had meant to borrow the landlady's iron the night before but somehow hadn't got round to it. Forgotten in a haze of sadness and alcohol.

But today was a hopeful day. Despite Bill's continued silence and cold absence, I hoped that this would be the day when everything turned around, when Bill, knowing it was my birthday today, would realise how wrong he'd been and come to see me. I had lain awake the night before, wishing and praying that he'd turn up today, with a small posy of flowers and a sheepish grin. I could almost see it in my mind, I could picture how I would take him in my forgiving arms. It felt so real, as though it really could happen, just as I'd found him again after all those years apart. We were meant to be. And even as I groaned with the nausea that made this morning difficult, I felt lighter and happier than I had for days.

I skipped down the stairs, reaching the front door of the building, and hunted for anything that resembled a birthday card. There were several brown envelopes, bills for the landlady, but nothing for me. I rarely got post, if ever. I had no family connections, no friends except for Una and a few other girls at work. The only other post I got was from Orla, one of my pals from Roscrea, but as time had gone on, and I'd moved about, even her letters were few and far between.

Perhaps he'll surprise me at work, like he used to, was the thought I cheered myself up with as I walked to the department store. Many times, Bill had met me after work, standing outside the back tradesmen entrance, greeting me with a wink and a kiss when I resurfaced after hours scrubbing plates. My heart physically ached when I remembered it.

All day, I kept glancing at the door, hoping I'd see him.

"What's got into ye, Biddy?" laughed Una, as she handed me yet another pile of dirty dishes.

"Ach nothing, I'm grand. Are we goin' out tonight? It is my birthday," I replied, smiling over at my friend.

"Sure, where would ye like to go?"

"I'd like to try the Irish bar again...." I said as casually as I could. I didn't want Una to know that the reason for going wasn't to enjoy a quiet drink with her, but to see if we could find Bill. It was the only other place I knew to look for him.

He'd never given me his address, and I didn't know his wife's name. The chances of finding him any other way were slim.

That night, Una and I stood at the bar. Even though it was a Friday, it was still early. I'd wanted to get there as soon as we could, and we were still dressed in our shabby work clothes rather than dressed up.

"I feel a terrible state!" laughed Una staring down at her brown shoes and navy skirt.

"Ach ye look grand, so ye do. You're a beauty Una, ye don't need fancy clothes or shoes to look like a princess!" I laughed.

Una shoved me playfully.

As she ordered the drinks I took advantage of the distraction, and looked around the bar, searching for his face at one of the round tables scattered round the edge of the pub. I couldn't see him.

We settled on our bar stools and soon the bar was full of rowdy men who'd finished their working week, and office girls in gaggles of three or four, batting their eyelids at them. I craned my neck trying to spot him.

As the evening wore on, I caught Una looking at me in a strange way. Of course she hadn't been taken in by casual suggestion that we return, for no particular reason, to the Irish bar.

"What is it?" I asked, knowing the answer already.

"Biddy, if I didn't know ye better, I'd think ye were tryin' to find that no-good sweetheart of yours. You know – the one who left ye in the family way…?" Una had been the first person I told when I realised I was pregnant. She'd warned me against telling Bill, but I'd ignored her advice. I didn't bother to deny it, Una knew me too well..

"He'll be here, I know he will. He knows it's my birthday. He knows this pub is special for us, so he'll be here," I said firmly, though I said it though gritted teeth.

Una sighed. "Look Biddy. I know ye love him, God knows how much you love that man, but I can tell ye now he isn't comin' back. He's back with his wife and kiddie, and there's nothing ye can do about it except move on with your life. You've got a baby of your own to think about now, and ye need to get some help from somewhere as you can't carry on workin' with a babe in your arms."

I didn't want to hear this. I ignored Una's wise words for the second time.

"I'm just goin' to the ladies. Don't get yourself into any more trouble while I'm gone," said my friend with a smile as she patted my hand.

When Una left I found myself standing up and moving towards the edge of the dance floor. In my mind's eye I could see Bill in front of me, his arms circling me, his lips mouthing his own words for our song. It was so potent, so real, it felt like he was actually there…

"Oh, sorry love!"

My eyes jerked open, momentarily confused. A solid-built man with tattoos on his forearm had shoved past me, spilling some of his beer on my skirt.

I blinked. The spell was broken. I saw that I was standing alone in a busy bar, surrounded by couples kissing, men and office girls flirting, people laughing and shouting, and I suddenly wanted to go. Without a word to Una, I fled. I part-ran, part-walked to the bus stop that would get me home to Coventry.

Once inside my room, I collapsed onto my bed in floods of tears. Bill wasn't coming back for me. I saw it now, really saw it – and a great black hole opened up in my heart. What sort of a fool was I, thinking he'd turn up just because it was my birthday? Jaysus, I was carrying his baby and that hadn't been enough to keep him by my side. When my sobs subsided I poured the last of the sherry into a cup until it almost overfilled and I drank it all in one go. I was alone, unmarried and pregnant. I was disgraced yet again, fooled by empty promises and deserted by a man who would forsake his own child rather than be with me.

Perhaps the priests and the nuns had been right? Perhaps I really was a sinner, hell-bent on self-destruction, a bad woman to whom bad things happened.

Perhaps I deserved everything I got. The thought made me reach for a bottle of beer I'd stashed under my bed. I had to drown these feelings, disconnect from the searing pain that squashed the air from my lungs and drove me into the pit of my own despair.

On May 17, 1956, I went into labour. I'd worked right up till my time, refusing to leave, and was only kept on because I worked in the back rooms so none of the 'respectable' shoppers might ever see me. My manageress had been unsympathetic, saying the rules were clear; as soon as the baby arrived I was dismissed, left to fend for myself in an increasingly hostile world.

"Don't worry, I'll drop by every week with a loaf of bread and some eggs," said Una. "You won't starve, Biddy. After all, I'll want to come and see the littl' one." I smiled gratefully at my good-hearted friend, but my mind felt paralysed with fear. I simply could not see how I would survive and care for my baby, and yet I did nothing in the face of this impending doom. It was like I was frozen in time, but time was rolling on. I couldn't seem to think straight, or do anything to help myself.

I finally gave birth to my daughter at 2am on Friday, May 18, at Gulson Hospital in Coventry. I had been put on Farren Ward, which was set aside for the Irish unmarried mothers, and was run by formidable Matron Howes.

I had managed to pull myself together in time for this moment and had stopped drinking when, after the initial shock of Bill's departure, I realised, once and for all, that he was gone for good. It was as though I suddenly woke up from the romantic dream that had paralysed me. It was time to face the sober truth that I was on my own, there was only one person respon-sible for the tiny life inside me. There was no place for self pity now. And if I didn't stop punishing myself, I would end up punishing this innocent little soul, too. It was the day, four months into my pregnancy, that I felt the first proper fluttering of the infant inside me, that was the moment I vowed to stop drinking and take care of myself properly, and in doing so, care for my unborn child. It was time to be a good mother.

"Here you go, Miss Larkin, your daughter." The matron handed me my little girl. I gazed down at her in wonder. This tiny bundle was part of the proof of my life going so wrong – but I couldn't feel anything but pure love and absolute joy at the sight of her. She had a tuft of blonde hair and blue eyes, just like Bill's. There was no doubt she was his daughter.

"Well if he can't be here to love ye, then what do we care? I'll give ye all the love ye need. I'm your mammy, and I'll look after ye and care for ye as long as I live…" I vowed.

As I smiled into my daughter's face, I swore she smiled back, even though the nurses told me babies didn't properly smile for weeks yet.

"Now, what shall I call ye, hey?' My baby gurgled with pleasure and I beamed with happiness as I watched her chubby little finger encircling mine.

"I'd call ye Philomena, but that's my sister's name, and I know I'll probably never see her again, so why don't I call ye, Phyllis. My littl' Phyllis. How d'ye like that for a name, huh?"

Little Phyllis yawned a contented yawn, and out of nowhere a nurse appeared and took her from me.

"Time for you both to rest," she said firmly. I didn't dare argue, though I was reluctant to hand her over after what happened with Kieran following his birth. This time was different, the nurses were kinder, but the trauma of my firstborn being taken from me had left me with a deep mistrust for anyone official. I watched as the nurse walked down the ward holding Phyllis, never for a moment taking my eyes off her.

Finally, I settled down, back into the pillows and the clean, crisp white sheets, preparing to doze, the smile never leaving my face.

Whatever anguish and heartbreak I'd been through in

leaving Kieran behind and losing my true love, it was nothing now compared to the love I felt for my daughter. I had no idea how I would cope, but I was determined to keep her and do right by her. She was my only family now. The reason I would go on living.

CHAPTER 16

LOSING LITTLE PHYLLIS
May 1956 to February 1957

"Ye can't take my baby, this time I won't let ye." I snatched Phyllis from her cot and held her in my arms, glowering at matron, and the woman from the Catholic adoption agency.

"They took my Kieran. You won't be gettin' my Phyllis. I'm going to raise her myself and to hell with the lot of ye." I stuck out my chin as I stood holding my daughter, glaring around the ward. They'd have to kill me before I'd let them take her from me. The midwife, a lady called Margaret, looked down at her hands, smiling.

"Well, I think Bridget is clear. She's going to bring up her child herself. There's nothing more we can do here."

She touched my shoulder as she walked past, a small show of solidarity. Matron tutted but she turned to the adoption lady and said: "We'll talk in my office." That was that. They all left the ward, leaving me standing, holding my child, unable to believe I'd stood up to the strict matron all by myself!

I looked around. There were two women who had signed the adoption papers sitting in nearby beds. Both were weeping. I had no clue how I would bring up Phyllis, how I would work and what would happen to us, but this time I was determined to try. I didn't want to be like those girls saying goodbye to their babies. I couldn't go through that again. Many of the mothers here were separated from their babies at birth. Matron would always say it was better that way as they wouldn't form close bonds, which would be severed by the eventual adoption, but to me, that felt cruel. From day one of Phyllis's life I insisted on feeding her with the bottle myself and cuddling her whenever I wanted. I had finally learned to stand up for myself. I was amazed when I was put into a separate room, usually kept for the mothers who were going home with their babies, and given the support of Miss Paton, the Moral Welfare Officer from St Faith's Shelter in Coventry, a home for 'fallen women'. Miss Paton would help me find new digs, come round for house visits and I'd even be given some financial help for the first few months until we were settled.

It was a dismal little bedsit that they found for us, but at least it was a roof over our heads. The day we moved in, I tried not to notice the nicotine-stained wallpaper and threadbare carpet. This was a new beginning and the only thing that mattered now was looking after my baby. The first few weeks were tough, but with enough money to pay my rent and buy food, I felt hopeful for the future.

I made sure that Phyllis's nappies were changed regularly, and she was fed whenever she was hungry. Miss Paton made a few attempts to come and see us, but every time the doorbell went I hid, shushing Phyllis in my arms, hoping Miss Paton would go away. To start with I'd been pleased to have so much support, but my old ways of thinking soon crept back and I started to fear that her attention was all a ruse to take Phyllis away from me. I still had difficulty trusting people in authority, and especially anyone linked to the church, after what happened with my son. In hindsight, not accepting the help Miss Paton offered me was a mistake. Left alone with no one to support me, my fears had taken hold of me and I slipped back into drinking again. It was a massive act of self destruction, made all the more bitter when I had done so well in staying off the booze for the sake of the little girl relying on me. But my addiction to alcohol was deep and my self control very fragile. The pregnancy and euphoria of having my beautiful daughter had really helped to cushion the pain of my latest, devastating loss. But now I was on my own again, facing an uncertain future, it didn't take much for the feelings of self hatred to kick in. Bill's betrayal of our love – and our child – had hit me harder than I realised.

I was completely broken by his desertion of us. These feelings came to the surface as I sat alone in my bedsit and so I reached for the one thing I knew would quickly ease my pain. My demons were back. Because I'd started drinking, I knew it was bad for the baby and for me, and it prompted me to withdraw yet further from the help offered to me. I didn't want Miss Paton to smell the alcohol on my breath. I didn't want her to see the mess my room was in, or how I was short of food because I'd spent my pennies on cheap cider and sherry. The days seemed ever longer, and soon I was trapped in my bedsit, with a crying, hungry baby, and my ever-present loneliness.

"Don't cry, my darlin'. Don't cry for your mammy." I would try to shush Phyllis, jiggling her in my arms, back and forth between window and bedstead to try and calm her, but nothing worked.

"Come on my angel. Be quiet for Mammy. Please settle down. Please just go to sleep," I begged as I paced, up and down, up and down, desperate for her to rest. My exhaustion was compounded by the relentless waking, feeding and changing cycle of my days and nights. I was snatching only a few hours of sleep in each 24 hours.

Every time I looked at her, I saw Bill's face. I wept every day for the loss of him, wondering if he would ever see our daughter, stroke her cheek, kiss her soft forehead. During the long, lonely hours, I would imagine Bill with his wife and child, a happy family man, while I was here, alone and missing him desperately, even though he'd let us down so cruelly.

Instead of daydreaming about a man who wasn't worthy of another thought, I should have been focusing on my own life and how to make it better. But I batted away the helping hand that was offered to me and my baby.

Letters arrived from the Moral Welfare Officer, official letters telling me to meet with her. I ignored them.

All night Phyllis howled and I wept.

I knew I needed to pull myself together, I had managed it when I was pregnant, but with a small baby and no sleep, with the loneliness and fear she'd be taken away, I found it so hard.

Eventually Miss Paton called round, and in a fog of tiredness I forgot my tough stance and let her in. She gasped as she surveyed the room.

"Bridget, this is in a terrible state. You've been drinking! There are bottles everywhere."

Pretty much the only time I went out these days was to buy more booze, taking Phyllis with me in the big perambulator that the shelter had let me borrow, wheeling her through the centre of Coventry.

I looked around my bedsit as if for the first time, seeing it through someone else's eyes. Without the routine of work or the company of others, I had sunk into a pit of despair that showed in my surroundings. I hadn't fully realised the squalor I was living in, nor quite how out of control my drinking had become. It was a cold November evening, Phyllis was sitting up at six months old, but I realised with alarm that I hadn't noticed the line of booze bottles on the shelf just above her, the dirty nappies in a bucket of cold water and piles of rags, clothing and general rubbish that had accumulated over the months.

I was so ashamed that I could not look Miss Paton in the eye. "I'm sorry, I'm just so tired," was all I could mutter by way of apology.

The Moral Welfare Officer surveyed me, then took control.

"Right, Bridget, we'll soon have this place shipshape. You entertain Phyllis and I'll get going with the washing."

Within an hour, the clothing was all folded and placed in the drawers. Phyllis's bed in the other drawer was cosy with a fresh blanket. The nappies in the stinking bucket had been boiled, and they were now hanging on the line that stretched across the room, dripping a little onto the floor. The empty bottles had been deposited by the bin outside, ready for collection by local kids who would no doubt take them back to the liquor stores for a few pennies.

"Right, well I'll be back next week. If you need anything, you must let us know."

And she left.

Things could've changed then. If there was ever a turning point, it should've been then, but my life, and my drinking, had spiralled out of control. I loved my daughter fiercely but the pull of sweet oblivion, the cravings for alcohol, seemed to override everything, even my feelings for my own flesh and blood. Even so, I made an attempt to turn things around by begging for some help. I had no family and no friends who could ease things for me, just for an hour here or there. In desperation, I put a small card in the local post office asking for a 'nice couple' to have Phyllis for a weekend so I could sleep. I didn't care that they would be strangers, I was at the end of my tether and I was desperate.

I was extremely lucky. The only people to respond were a lovely couple called Mr and Mrs Curran who took Phyllis every week from Friday through to Sunday. Kind, warm and reliable, the Currans already had one daughter, aged seven, and they told me that "God in his wisdom had seen fit to only bless them with the one child." So they poured all of their abundant love into the care of others, including Phyllis, whom they doted on. They loved my daughter so much, they told me they would consider adopting her if I couldn't cope. But I snatched her back, making it clear that, no matter what, I would never, ever, give up my baby.

December arrived and when I realised I had no money to buy Phyllis even a small present, I broke down, knowing what little money I had I needed for booze, just in order to get through the day. I was putting alcohol above my own daughter and I felt powerless to do anything about it. I was wretched, filled with self disgust but I didn't know where to turn or what to do to stop the ruinous cycle.

Then another letter arrived, this time from Canon William Flint, giving me an appointment to meet with another officer at the Birmingham Diocesan Rescue Society for the Protection of Homeless and Friendless Catholic Children in Coleshill, Birmingham – or Father Hudson's Homes as it was more commonly known. I sat looking at the words, wondering if this was the help I needed, thinking I had to do something to save us.

On Tuesday, December 11, 1956, I wheeled Phyllis to the station and caught the train to Birmingham, where I changed for Coleshill. It was a short walk to the rescue society, but I dawdled, feeling apprenhensive. Did they want to take Little Phyllis from me, just like Kieran had been taken?

Walking into Miss May McFadden's office, I was greeted by the Moral Welfare Officer, who was like a strict headmistress, very assertive and a little intimidating. Despite this, she smiled at me. She was dressed in a pristine white blouse and navy skirt, and flat shoes with her hair tied back in a bun. Her office was clean and tidy and it had a strong smell of wax polish. There was a large bookcase on the one wall and on the other wall there was a wooden crucifix, it certainly didn't have a homely feel about it. There was, however, a lovely view of the garden from the large window.

"Come and sit down, dear," she said, pointing to a chair. There were a few baby toys, a doll made out of stuffed material and a tin spinning top. I put Phyllis down and she grabbed for the doll.

"Now, the reason we've asked you here is because we're worried about you and your daughter. It seems our colleagues at the St Faith Shelter have been largely unable to keep track of you."

I looked away. I didn't want an interrogation.

The woman cleared her voice.

"It seems to me, well to all of us, that you are struggling, Bridget. Would I be right in saying that?"

I gulped, tears prickling my eyes, then nodded.

I couldn't speak. I was overcome with emotion as I finally acknowledged my helpless despair. I looked at my daughter chewing the hair of the doll and knew I couldn't cope by myself. I didn't have the ability to be a mammy, I could barely look after myself, let alone the most precious thing in the world to me.

"We'd like to offer you both somewhere to live with us at our centre in Liverpool. I'm afraid we don't have mothers staying with their babies here. What do you say to that?"

Suddenly, I was overcome with fear. What I knew of mother and baby homes was Roscrea, where they took my son away after just six days. I wouldn't let that happen to Phyllis.

'No!' I cried. "I don't need your help. I don't need anyone's help. If I live with you in a mother and baby home ye'll take little Phyllis from me."

I stood up, grabbed my daughter and marched out of that place, not once looking back.

A few days later, I received a copy of a letter sent by Miss McFadden to my parish priest Father Basil Griffin. He had baptised Phyllis on July 8, 1956, at St Osburgs RC Church in Hill St, Coventry. I rarely, if ever, went to Mass, but on the rare occasions I did, I turned to the priest for advice. I wanted my daughter to be brought up a Catholic, even though I had been traumatised by the church's treatment of me. I was confused about how I felt about my religion, but it was still at the heart of my life simply because it always had been.

14th December, 1956

Dear Father Basil,
Re: Bridget Larkin, 7 Byron St, Coventry.
This girl called to see me on Tuesday and said that she had seen you and that you would be writing on her behalf.

From the interview it would appear that the only satisfactory solution for her is to offer accommodation for herself and her baby. A home in Liverpool would be suitable so that she, too, could have care and protection, which she seems to need.

She will only come to more trouble if left to herself.

Unfortunately, Bridget was not in the least bit prepared to take this offer of help and so, alas there is little else that I can do for her.

Yours very sincerely,

Miss May McFadden *(Moral Welfare Officer)*

I stared down at the letter, unable to sort out my thoughts. On one hand I knew the church was trying to help and support me, and I was grateful for it. On the other hand, I was so devastated by what had happened to me at Roscrea, that I couldn't bring myself to accept it. Who has the right to steal a baby from their mother? Instead of gratitude I felt rage building inside me. Who were these do-gooders to decide what was best for me and my daughter? Even as I reacted with anger, a part of me knew I had few other choices but to let myself be supported. Yet I was too scarred by the tragedy of losing Kieran. How could I describe the unbearable agony of leaving my son on his own, without his mammy. I couldn't even bring myself to respond to this insult of a letter. I ripped it into small pieces and slugged down the rest of my bottle of beer. My head was woozy.

Phyllis was crying but I didn't have the energy to pick her out of the drawer where she'd been sleeping but had evidently awoken. I lay on my bed, curling my body into the foetal position and lay there, staring at the wall as the tears ran and ran down my face. Both Phyllis and I cried ourselves to sleep.

***

Standing at the entrance to Father Hudson's home in Coleshill again, I almost bolted. Looking down at Phyllis who was wrapped up in warm blankets, cooing to herself in the pram, I wanted to grab her and run. But where I would take her was anybody's guess. All my plans to keep her, to raise my own child, were defeated. I loved my daughter, had fought the authorities desperately hard to keep her, yet here I was, seconds before I handed her over to the Moral Welfare Officer for adoption. I had lost the fight of my life. Months of refusing entrance to the officer, refusing any help offered had played out, and there was nowhere left for Phyllis and me to go. Miss Paton had written to Canon Flint, and between them they'd organised that she would accompany me to Father Hudson's home so that Little Phyllis could be admitted into the nursery.

It was the hardest decision I have ever faced in my life, but by then I knew I was drowning – Phyllis deserved better than me and the life I could give her.

In the past three months, I knew I'd been struggling to look after my little girl. I often forgot to change her, left her crying or felt too sad or overwhelmed to leave the grimy bedsit for days at a time, except to buy beer. I knew, too, that this was no life for my beloved child. It was brought home to me one morning as I hunted for something warm to wrap Phyllis in while we took a walk out to buy my daily supplies; milk for the baby and beer for me. I couldn't find her hat so we went out without it. It was a cold day. I stepped outside and realised that every baby we passed on the way to the shops was wearing a bonny woollen hat. I looked at Phyllis. Her face was dirty, her unwashed cardigan smelled of stale milk and her cheeks were pink with cold because she had no hat. I knew in that moment I was failing her.

I also knew I was referred to by neighbours and the officers as a 'drunk'. On the rare occasions I did let a midwife or social worker into my squalid home, I could see the shock register on their faces at the empty bottles, the mess and the dirt; all of it evidence that I couldn't cope. I had a wholehearted distrust of authority but as I looked at my daughter that morning, in her dirty clothes and without her hat, I realised this was down to me. It was time for me to stop blaming others and to take responsibility. As her mother, I could not even keep her clean and warm.

I finally admitted to myself that she would be better cared for with a proper family, in a better neighbourhood and with a mother who didn't spend all her waking time thinking about drink.

So here I was, at 3pm on February 22, 1957, about to give up my precious second child for adoption. It was a date that would be forever embedded in my memory. How had it come to this? Had fate been cruel or was it no more than I deserved? Either way, I felt my heart was breaking.

Earlier that day, I had packed a small suitcase for nine-month-old Phyllis, carefully placing inside her woolly cardigans and clean nappies, together with her only toy, a small teddy bear.

I sighed as I slowly, methodically tucked them all inside her devastating going-away bag. *I won't cry today. I won't cry,* I repeated in my mind, though it was a vow I'd find impossible to keep.

I'd made Phyllis a warm mush of milk and mashed potatoes for breakfast, it was her favourite food and she had guzzled it down happily. She was always happy. And though food was sometimes a bit late in coming, I always made sure Phyllis had enough to eat, even when I didn't. My daughter was a plump, sweet little thing with a sunny disposition. Looking at her smiling, trusting little face, my chest hurt with stifled sobs, but I didn't want her to see me upset. I wanted her last experience with me at home to be a happy one, even if she was too young to ever remember it.

"I popped a few tatties in my pocket when I went down to pay my rent," I giggled as I spooned food into her mouth. "What she don't see, she don't miss."

I knew it was wrong to steal but I wanted to give my daughter a proper meal as a send-off. I promised myself it was the last time I'd filch from the unsuspecting dragon who ran the lodgings, and I meant it, even though the 'dragon' was a mean-spirited lady who periodically threatened to make me homeless because of the baby crying, and who never smiled in the whole time I knew her. My room was damp, and the landlady refused to do anything about it. It was grimy, cold and had black mould growing up one wall. So maybe I shouldn't feel too bad about nicking a few tatties for my baby girl.

Time moved on relentlessly. I played with Phyllis all morning, my eye constantly returning to the clock face. I couldn't stop touching her. I inhaled the top of her head, stroked her plump little cheeks, blew raspberries on her tummy; I tried to drink in every inch of her in those precious few moments. I couldn't think about what came next.

We reached Father Hudson's home via a taxi that the charity paid for. I made my way with Miss Paton inside to the main office. Miss McFadden was there, as was Canon Flint.

"Bridget has forgotten her milk tokens and Phyllis's medical card. But I'm sure she has had other things on her mind," said Miss Paton. I looked at the floor. It seemed I had failed even this, the handover of my child.

"Are we ready then, Bridget? Have you said goodbye?"
I reached into the pram and pulled out Phyllis, snuggling her

up to me and kissing her pink cheeks.

"I'll be back for ye one day, I promise ye Littl' Phyllis," I whispered, breathing in her baby smell, trying to hold the memory of it inside me. "I won't leave you here, when my life's better I'll be back, ye'll see. I'm your mammy and I'll never forget ye, d'ye hear me?" I didn't know how I would get through the next few seconds.

Miss McFadden handed me a pink cardigan.

"The girls all have pink, the boys have blue. You might want to dress her in that and then hand her to me," she said.

I took the cardie, placed Phyllis on my knees and dressed her with trembling fingers. Phyllis looked up at me and smiled, a toothless gummy smile – and it was at that point what I was doing hit home. My heart broke. It shattered in my chest. I felt sick and faint, and the room started to spin.

The Moral Welfare Officer must've seen my distress as she quickly took Phyllis from my arms, and without another word, bustled out of the room, chatting brightly to my daughter as she was taken from me. My arms felt suddenly light as air, and memories of my last cuddle with Kieran flooded back.

Canon Flint stood up. His face was sad rather than alarmed. He must have witnessed hundreds of mothers being separated from their children, just like me.

He made to say something, but I didn't want to hear it. I didn't want platitudes. I knew my daughter would be better off without me as her mammy but that only served to intensify the heartbreak I was feeling. It was all my fault.

I thrust Phyllis's suitcase into his hand and I fled, forcing back the sobs that racked my body until I had left that place. Not caring who saw me, I ran all the way to the train station – there was no taxi for me this time –and jumped onto a train heading out of Coleshill. The journey back was a blur. I spent it weeping, my body shuddering with the force of my anguish.

"Are you alright, dearie?" asked an elderly woman. I didn't reply. I had no words.

The worst had happened to me and who could I blame if not myself? I was a mother twice over and I had lost two children. I had experienced catastrophe after catastrophe. The only comfort I had was found in a bottle of grog and I knew that the booze was partly what had brought me here. I also knew, with a terrible sinking feeling, that oblivion was the only way I'd ever escape the pain of the loss that was tearing me apart.

CHAPTER 17
A LIFE UNRAVELS
Christmas 1957 to September 1963

"After Phyllis's dad, anyone will do. If I can't have him, I won't be choosy, I don't care, and that's the truth!" As I slammed down my glass, its contents sloshed all over the bar top.

"Go on, Biddy, you tell it like it is!" cackled the bedraggled man propping up the bar next to me.

"I'll have ye any time, Biddy, ye just give me the nod and the wink!" shouted another.

I laughed along with them, but inside I felt numb. It was Christmas 1957, 10 months after I'd walked out of Father Hudson's home, leaving with empty arms and an aching heart. From the day I'd left, I barely had a night without drinking and the days and evenings had blurred into chaos. I'd lost my latest job washing up in a pub because I was always late, or sometimes never showed up at all. But my lack of cash never stopped me from getting a drink.

"Ach, I've spilt my beer... which one of you nice men will buy me another?" I lurched over to a different man, one with nicer clothes and smelling of cologne.

"I'll buy ye another Biddy, don't ye worry, girl. Stick with me," he joked and put his arm around me. I knew his face. He'd been in the bar a few times recently and I'd liked the look of him.

"You'll do!" I countered, bursting into song as the pianist struck up the first notes of a popular sing-along.

"What a girl ye are, Biddy. Always the life and soul of the party eh!"

I looked again at this man. He seemed nice, with twinkly eyes and just a hint of the blarney about him.

"I'm always happy, me, don't ye forget it."

The Irish bar, in a seedy back street in Birmingham city centre, was filled up with the rowdiest punters for miles around, all drinking on Christmas Eve. There was always a song being sung or a drink to be had at a stranger's behest. I came here because it stopped me thinking about how lonely my life was, how sad and frightened I felt in the long overnight hours. Saying I was always happy was a lie, I just diluted my despair with booze. It was the festive season, I had no responsibilities and was responsible to no one, and I kidded myself I was having the height of fun.

Of course, what I really yearned for was a man and a baby to love. I had messed around with a stream of men, many of whom just wanted to sleep with me then disappear. Each time I met someone I'd think, "Here he is, the one that'll replace Bill", and yet it never worked out that way. It was patently obvious to anyone that my life was unravelling fast. I worked in various menial jobs but always got sacked in the end. I'd tell myself they always had too many rules, they just didn't want you to have any fun. That's an alcoholic's logic for you.

"Snuggle up to me, love, and I'll keep ye warm. I'm Sean."

I smiled a wonky, drunken smile, and handed him my glass. I saw by the look in his eye that I wouldn't be alone tonight, and that was enough for me.

***

"Ach, my head…" I groaned as I came around. My whole body ached. I was lying on something hard and cold and very definitely not my bed. It took me a few seconds to realise I was laying on the floor of a police cell.

"Help! Get me out of here this instant!!" I yelled, wiping the spittle from my mouth. I smelt sour, reeking of alcohol and sick – I must've been ill on the booze the previous night.

I banged on the door. "Get me out of here ye brutes!"

"Ay ay she's awake, our resident duchess will be wanting her carriage and horses." The policeman chuckled as he unlocked my cell.

"Come on then, let's be having you. You made quite a scene last night, but I bet you don't remember a thing." He was tall, with an immaculate uniform and he raised an eyebrow at me, reminding me of one of the stricter nuns at school.

"Who d'ye think you are, holding me prisoner? Let me out this minute." I grumbled, following behind him as he marched me to the desk.

The policeman only chuckled again in response.

'Look here, Tipperary Mary, we're getting fed up of the sight of you here. Now, I know it's Christmas, and we all like a tipple at this time of year, but it's becoming a habit, don't you think?" The chap was tall and fair and rather handsome. In fact, he reminded me of the person I was trying, so unsuccessfully to forget.

"Do you have any recollection of last night?" he said, this time seriously. I looked down at my skirt, which I noticed was ripped, and at the mess I was in. I shook my head. I knew I'd met a nice man at the bar on Christmas Eve, or at least I thought I did, but what happened after that was lost in my blackout. And now I was here, on Christmas Day, at the police station. I had no idea how I got there and, given the state I was in, I didn't really want to know.

The man sighed. "We're not going to charge you with anything, though you came dangerously close to being arrested for being drunk and disorderly. I strongly advise you to seek help for your drinking. You can go, but don't let me see you here again."

I kept my head down, my face smarting with the humiliation, as I grabbed my bag and ran out of the station. I was in Birmingham, so that was good, I hadn't gone far.

"Bridget, you'll get a meal at St Chad's hostel down the road," said the fair-haired copper, who had followed me out and was standing on the station steps. "Go and get yourself some hot food."

"I don't need charity," I huffed. But when I looked back at the policeman he was smiling kindly at me. "Just for today Bridget, it's Christmas."

I knew where the hostel was, and I found my feet taking me there, even as my brain was telling me that I surely hadn't sunk so low.

I hovered by the door but couldn't bring myself to step over the threshold. I didn't want to sit with a lot of stinking, toothless, cider-sodden down and outs. I may be low but I was better than that. Wasn't I? As I turned to go, the door opened and a cheery voice called, "Would you like to come in? We have some turkey going spare." I turned round and was met with a warm round face – grinning at me. Just what I need, I thought miserably, a cheerful do-gooder… "My name's Alison," said the owner of the grin. "Why don't you come in and at least get warm."

So I did. And while it won't go down on record as the best Christmas Day ever, it did turn out to be not bad at all. We sat around a long table, pulled crackers, ate turkey and, with some encouragement from the volunteers serving our food, even wore paper hats. We were a motley collection of diners: the old, the young, men and women. We didn't share life stories. It was clear that some of the diners were familiar with one another and I recognised a couple of faces from the hardcore drinkers who sometimes went to the Irish pub. One of them called out to me, his mouth full of food: "Hey, Tipperary Mary, where's me Christmas present?"

"I'll give ye a present all right if ye don't stop spittin' sprouts in our faces."

Everyone laughed and I laughed along with them. A couple of us helped with the washing up and then Alison said that the volunteers were going to give us a little carol concert. My head was splitting and I was dying for a drink but, with nothing better to do and no place else to go, I sat along with everyone else and even attempted to join in with the chorus of Silent Night. But as I started to sing, I could feel the sobs rising up and I knew once I started I'd never stop weeping – for my babies and the pathetic tragedy that was my life. I stayed there the night, grateful for the warmth and the company. I didn't want to be alone with my thoughts that night and besides, I had no way of getting home. Alison handed me a mug of cocoa and said, "It's a new year soon Mary and I wish you a very happy one."

I didn't bother to tell her that my name was Bridget. I was Tipperary Mary to everyone else now. Despite not having a drop to drink, I fell into a deep sleep.

The next day, the policeman's words beat inside my brain: 'Get help for your drinking'. Did I need help? Wasn't it more the case that I got carried away now and then? More than that, if I stopped drinking, what pleasure would my life contain? I shut down that thought as fast as it came.

I was fine. I'd had a hard life – and a tipple or two was the only way I got to relax and enjoy myself.

On the way home, I found a pound note in the street and immediately spent it on a bottle of cider. I took it home and drank until I reached that comforting, hazy place where nothing really mattered. I lay on the narrow bed, knowing that the next day I would hate myself all over again for letting the booze get the better of me. But for now I could sink into oblivion. I drank some more until I was able to drift off to sleep while telling myself that one day things would get better. One day, I'd have a babe in my arms that I could keep and cherish…

Deep in my heart I knew that no amount of drink would heal my crippling loneliness or my longing to love and be loved. The hole left by Kieran and then Phyllis had only grown in the months since I'd fled Father Hudson's home. I had been back once so far, a couple of months earlier in October.

I'd had to write requesting a visit, which was granted and I was issued with a visiting pass by Miss McFadden. But seeing Phyllis again had triggered an avalanche of loss, and I only stayed for a few minutes, it was too painful seeing her. Holding my child made me want another. I don't know if it was a desperate urge to have someone to love or whether Mother Nature kicked in again but even though I'd had to give up my second baby, I still wanted a child of my own. It didn't make any sense. Although it would have destroyed me to admit it, I knew I'd lost forever my chance to keep Phyllis. But holding her made me long for another chance, another baby, with a clean slate. And this time with a man who loved us both.

I hadn't been back to see my daughter since then, though I'd promised her I would return regularly. I kept thinking I'd go as soon as I sorted myself out, but it got to Friday and the lure of the bars was too strong, and very often I didn't make it home until Sunday. It was on those post-binge days when, hungover and feeling wretched, I cried tears of self pity while telling myself I didn't deserve to have my sweet little girl.

Then one Saturday in Spring 1958, I decided to go and see my Little Phyllis again.

It was an unseasonably warm day and I was carried on a wave of optimism. I put on my hat, a red cloche beret, and coat and looked at myself in the mirror. The excesses of my life were becoming harder to hide but I was still young, and when I smiled my face lit up still, though I had less and less to feel joy about.

Before I go I'll just have a swig of sherry to calm my nerves, I said to myself, reaching for the bottle that was always next to my bed, reminding me of my mammy.

Perhaps I should have another, just to see me through, I muttered, pouring a second cup.

By the time I walked through Coventry to catch a bus to Coleshill, I was feeling unsteady. I had to hold on to some railings at one point as I felt faint. I'd eaten nothing that morning, nor any tea the night before, so the sherry was the only sustenance I'd had. I'd brought the dregs of the bottle with me, for courage, and when I stopped I made sure to finish it, leaving the bottle next to the railings.

The bus conductor looked at me strangely but accepted my proffered coins and I made my way to the nearest seat. The woman I sat next to stood up abruptly, tutting as she went to find another seat.

"I don't mind, I've got more room now," I declared, with fake bravado. I remembered a lullaby I had sung to my babies, one I remembered from my own childhood, and sang it to myself on the journey.

I turned to the woman behind me, wanting to tell her where I was going and perhaps have a chat – it felt so long since I'd talked to anyone. But she wasn't interested, she averted her gaze and pretended I wasn't there.

Upon entering the familiar building I was, by now, worse for wear, but I attempted to put my best foot forward.

"Wait here, please," said the lady at the office, and so I sat, listening to the clock tick, remembering another office in Ireland where I'd waited. I was on the point of leaving. My stomach turned over, I felt sick and woozy and suddenly very scared to see my daughter.

"Here she is, but we can only let you have a couple of minutes with her, and we'll stay here with you both," said a nun without smiling. Another elderly nun had my daughter Phyllis in her arms.

I stood up too fast, swaying as I did so.

"My darlin', my Littl' Phyllis. It's your mammy. I told ye I'd come back, didn't I?"

I could feel the tears streaming down my face. The nun looked pointedly at the other sister, but I wasn't sure why.

"Come here, come to Mammy…" I held out my arms, and the sister reluctantly handed her over.

"Have you been drinking, Miss?" she asked quietly.

I ignored her, concentrating instead on trying to grasp one of my daughter's podgy little fingers.

"Shall I sing ye a lullaby like I used to? D'ye remember when it was just us together?" I slurred. Phyllis looked at me, uncertain now, her face confused and a little fearful.

My daughter was not yet two years old, and I saw for the first time that she had forgotten me already. I started to cry, squeezing Phyllis as I wept, rocking her in my grief. Now the nuns looked alarmed.

"Oh my goodness!" one of them exclaimed. The other came forward and prised Phyllis out of my arms. She had started to cry and I realised I'd probably frightened her.

"Bring her back, I didn't mean to upset her. She's my girl, my baby…" I cried, but the nun left the room and I knew I couldn't follow.

I stared bleakly at the other nun who was still in the room. "Let me get you a glass of water, then I think it's best you leave," she said.

I nodded.

It had been a mistake coming here. Phyllis no longer knew me as her mammy. To her I was a stranger, and the knowledge broke my heart.

Five months later, in October 1958, I woke up with a familiar jolt in my belly and retched into the bucket I kept by my bed. I hadn't been drinking the night before, so I was confused, thinking I must have a bug.

As I was lying there, I suddenly knew it wasn't a stomach upset. It had been two months since my 'monthlies' had come – how could I have been so stupid not to notice the signs. I was pregnant again!

This time, I'm ashamed to say, I didn't know who the father was. I'd carried on with Sean and with another fella I met in the bars. I didn't even know the name of the other man.

He'd pretended to comfort me one night in the pub when I was crying for my babies, and he took me outside 'for air' where he pushed me up against the gully wall and had sex with me. I knew he wanted sex and nothing else; by then I was numb to everything except the pain of losing my children. But for a few brief minutes it made me feel wanted.

Neither man had wanted to settle down with me, and I guess I was happy to make do with the pleasure of a night's companionship and someone to cuddle me in bed and, well, the rest that came with having a man in my bed.

"Jaysus, how did I miss this...what have I done? Mary, Mother of God, help me." I stared over at the plaster image of Our Lady, which sat by the stove. It was a small, cheap version, like the kind sold in the penny bazaars.

I still went to Mass when I was sober enough to go. It gave me some relief from my troubles, but after Roscrea I still struggled to rediscover my relationship with God and the Catholic Church. So much wrong had been done to me in its name. It was no wonder my faith was sorely tested – and found wanting.

I muttered a prayer, begging for help, but I knew the signs. I was pregnant with no man beside me, just like before.

Heaven couldn't help me now.

I gave birth to Angela on June 2, 1959, at Gulson Hospital in Coventry, by which point I'd changed my surname to Ryan, Bill's surname. By then I risked being sent back to Ireland by the police as I'd been in trouble so many times, and they only knew me by my name 'Larkin'. I think in my mind I still longed for Bill, to be his wife, and taking his name felt like I was a step closer to him. Silly though it seems, I needed to keep an ember of hope alive.

Changing my name was also an attempt to sever my

connection to my family in Ireland, to put my dark past behind me, though it didn't work. Angela was three months old when she was taken into emergency foster care. The landlady of The Three Shoes pub, my local in Coventry, reported me to Social Services after I popped out for a quick drink, leaving Angela alone in her drawer in my lodgings. The police and Social Services arrived that very night. By the time they banged on the door I was home but drunk. I let them in and watched, confused, as they scooped up my daughter and carried her out of my home. I tried to shout but my words slurred and my head felt thick. When they left, I slumped onto my bed, weeping with contrition. How had I lost another child? Why couldn't I pull myself together, give up the drink and become the mother I was so desperate to be? Once again I was full of self loathing and guilt.

From then on I was only allowed supervised contact with Angela for an afternoon every fortnight. Shortly afterwards I visited the parish priest and Miss Paton and it was decided that a middle-aged couple, Mr and Mrs O'Brien, would become Angela's foster parents. They were from Ireland but had moved to Coventry for work. They had two older children of their own, and that at least gave me some comfort. My daughter would be part of a good Catholic family, and she would have from them the stability I seemed unable to give her.

In 1960, Canon Flint arranged for Phyllis to be adopted. I never went back to Father Hudson's after that last episode, partly out of shame, and partly out of sadness. The adoption order was made by a judge in Birmingham Juvenile Court in July of that year. Canon Flint was present to identify my daughter as I hadn't attended any of the hearings. I ignored it and pretended it wasn't happening; I couldn't bring myself to think about what was taking place.

I knew there was no point in putting up a fight for her: a lone, troubled – and let's say it, drunken – young woman like me stood no chance against the church and state. And part of me knew that I didn't really deserve another chance. I had abandoned Phyllis and I had watched as Social Services had, not unreasonably, removed Angela from me. I would never, ever be able to forgive myself for my failure as a mother. But that didn't stop me from repeating the same, shameful behaviour all over again as I continued on my self-destructive, downward spiral.

I carried on drinking and carousing. Two years on I woke up one morning with a man beside me and no recollection of how he came to be there. I had kicked him out but he had left me with a memento of our night together: I was pregnant. In January 1962 I gave birth to Billy, also at Gulson Hospital. My son was immediately taken into foster care, joining the same family who had fostered Angela. I had access visits to see both Angela and Billy, which was a step forward as I'd only seen Phyllis twice and Kieran not at all.

The anticipation of seeing them both, combined with the guilt I felt over them being taken from me, meant I was generally half-cut, if not completely drunk, by the time the visits took place. I couldn't cope with seeing them though I missed them desperately, so I drank to drown my nerves, to quiet my shame. I turned up sozzled so many times that my contact was dropped to once a month. There were times I didn't show up at all, the drink getting the better of me.

I did my best not to ruin this arrangement as the years passed, but when they got older, I couldn't help myself turning up at the gates at St Osburg's Catholic Primary School in Upper Hill

Street, shouting for them to come home with me. I will never forget the faces of my wide-eyed children looking at me like I was an alien from another planet. Many times I was escorted out of the building, sobbing and cursing, promising to change my ways, filled with regrets, but it did no good. Unsurprisingly, their foster mother reported me to the police and Social Services and all contact was stopped. I'd messed it up again, and God knows how it affected Angela and Billy. I later found out that they'd begged their foster mother to put a stop to my visits because they were so distressing for them. I'll admit it, by now I was nothing short of a tramp, with dirty, ragged clothing, odd socks and a pair of slippers for shoes. I sometimes slept rough as every landlady turned me out eventually.

Jimmie was born in August 1963 at the Birmingham Maternity Hospital.

His birth certificate, like those of all my children, stated 'father unknown'. By then I had moved to Birmingham to try and outrun my shame at being pregnant again. I couldn't face the nurses at Gulson Hospital tutting at me as I went into labour yet again. The move didn't really make any sense as I was known throughout the city centre as 'Tipperary Mary', never without a drink in her hand, but I just knew I was embarrassed to be having my third child since Phyllis with neither a groom nor a wedding ring in sight.

***

"Bill... Bill... BILL!" I ran faster than I ever had in my life, out of the bar and into Hurst Street.

"Biiiiilllll!" I screamed, as I watched the blond man walk to the end of the street and turn right up to New Street Station.

I cantered up the road, my heart beating.

It was him! After all this time, after all this disappointment, I was looking at the only man I had ever loved.

Then I spotted her. A woman walked up to him. Just at that moment, the man turned to kiss her and I could see that I was mistaken. It wasn't Bill. I didn't know if I felt relieved that he wasn't with another woman, or devastated – most likely a combination of the two emotions. I doubled over, panting and sweating. I could have sworn the man was my Bill, he was so alike him in every way.

Just then a hand grabbed my shoulder.

"Oi get off me!" I snarled as the policeman swung me round.

"Come with me," was all he said. I blinked at him for a moment, the force of the beer swilling about inside me stopped me from moving.

He gripped my shoulder tighter and I started to walk. Why had a policeman chased after me?

Jimmie! Jaysus Christ, I had left Jimmie in the pub. My senses cleared and I realised I was in deep trouble. Not for the first time I felt scalding hot shame. I'd left my own baby in the pub to run after the man who had broken my heart – and it hadn't even been him. What was wrong with me? Why did I get everything so very wrong?

"Oh Jaysus, officer I'm so sorry. I didn't mean to leave him. I love Jimmie, he's my baby boy," I pleaded. The officer didn't respond.

We reached the bar and Jimmie was where I'd left him in his pram. He was just a few weeks old, and I'd run out on him.

"Follow me to the station."

The policeman called the Child Protection Team and soon I was answering questions. But despite the searing hot tea placed in front of me, I couldn't seem to formulate the answers, my head spun, my lips were dry and all I could think about was how I'd left my baby boy.

I kept repeating, over and over: "I love him, I love him," but it made no difference. Jimmie was taken from me. He was put into care and adopted and there was nothing to be done. I had messed up yet another chance to love and be loved. All I could do was crawl back to my hovel and drink away the sadness until I passed out in a fog of recriminations and regrets.

CHAPTER 18
"MY NAME'S TIPPERARY MARY"
November 1964 to June 1973

My body was racked with pain. Clutching my stomach, I rolled over on my bed.

That's when I saw the red stain bloom across the sheet. I forced myself up and staggered to the bathroom down the hallway, hoping that my new landlady Mrs McGuire wouldn't yet be up snooping about as she always did, intent on poking her nose into my business.

Left pregnant by a man I probably wouldn't recognise in the street if I saw him again, my drinking had got worse, if anything, and this was the result; another unplanned pregnancy by an unknown father, except it was clear I was losing the baby.

I had been kicked out of my lodgings again a couple of months earlier. I hadn't been able to keep up with my rent and that, alongside my drunken rantings and rages, meant I'd had to pace the streets on a cold October evening in 1964.

With a few bags slung over my shoulders, I knocked at what felt like every door in Small Heath, Birmingham, as I'd been told there were always lodgings going there, in the cheapest part of the city. I'd had no luck and the sky was darkening, my stomach growling with hunger, when an elderly lady, Mrs McGuire, opened her door and led me inside to a back room in her bleak-looking terraced house.

"Ye'll be cosy and warm here, so ye will," said Mrs McGuire.

216

She was a small, grey-haired Irish matron, who permanently wore black in mourning for her husband and only child, a son who had died of rickets. I looked around the tiny space: a single iron bed stood to the side next to an open fireplace, the walls were stained brown and the windows looked like they'd never been opened. I had no choice but to take it.

"I can pay ye the rent tomorrow, so I'll just be goin' out to find my bearings," I said. "I won't keep you up late."

Before Mrs McGuire could respond, I hurried past her, pulling my coat around me and heading back out of the front door in the direction of one of the pubs that lined the street. As I walked I passed various shops and a scrap yard. It was clearly a poor area, and many of the dwellings weren't far off being slum tenements. Perhaps to take the sting out of the hard lives of those that lived and worked there, there were a fair few pubs sprinkled along the street.

I pushed open the door of the liveliest and the fullest pub. I squeezed past the punters, many of whom looked like 'tatters' or beggars, and found myself at the bar. I didn't have any money but that was never too much of a problem for a woman, even though I was now 35 years old and any looks I once possessed had been eaten away by the booze.

"Let me have a drink on the strap," I said to the barman, who raised his eyebrows. "You want a drink on credit? But I don't even know you. I haven't seen you before, where have you crawled out from?" he said, causing a few of the regulars at the bar to wheeze with laughter.

"I haven't crawled out of anywhere, thank ye very much, and I'd be grateful for that drink if ye please."

"She's got spirit and she's an Irish lass so she's one of us," said one of the men.

"And she's not bad looking." said another. "Go on, Sid, give her a drink, she can sit here with us."

The barman grabbed a glass and poured out a beer, placing it in front of me. I drank down the frothy liquid in one, slammed it down and said: "Another!"

The men at the bar cheered.

"What's your name, pet?" said one, a short fat man with a tuft of ginger hair and an accent that sounded more like Geordie than Irish.

"My name's Tipperary Mary, and don't ye forget it." I countered, bringing the second drink to my lips and smiling.

From then on I was a regular at the 'Tatters Arms' as we called it, because anyone, even a 'tatter' could get credit for a drink there. It was the reason it was so busy.

The Tatters Arms was full most nights of the week, and I knew that because I was always there. I knew my landlady was getting fed up of me staggering in late.

She'd threatened to call the police several times because of my unpaid rent and general bad behaviour but hadn't yet done it.

That morning, I managed to swab the blood with some rags and clean myself up a little. My head was pounding with yet another hangover and I found myself crying into my hands as I remembered the words of that policeman telling me to ease off the alcohol. Every morning my hands and body would shake until I could get that first drink inside me, when the tremors would stop and I'd start feeling 'human' again. It wasn't the right way to go about things, I knew it, yet I couldn't stop. I remembered what a pathetic figure my mammy made with her cup of sherry and permanent drunken fog and I knew I was going the same way, yet the itch to keep drinking, to block my memories and feelings, was too strong, so each night I drank, and each morning I regretted it and vowed to myself that I'd stop.

"My God, what has happened to ye?" Mrs McGuire's sharp eyes picked out the bloodstains on my nightie, the way I walked with a waddle due to the packing between my legs as she caught me leaving the bathroom. I'd only lived there a month but she had eyes like a hawk, watching me all the time.

"I lost a baby. It's nothin', I'm fine." I replied, banging my door in her keen face.

By lunchtime the police, a doctor, and I were sat in my room.

"You must undergo sterilisation. It's the only way forward for you, Miss Ryan," said the doctor.

I looked down at my hands in my lap.

"You must see that you can't cope with motherhood. Your drinking is out of control. We are trying to help you, but you must let us."

I shook my head, replying with venom: "I will not be sterilised! I'm a Catholic, it is strictly forbidden!"

The professionals all looked at each other. It was clear what they thought of my moral code, but I was adamant.

"I may not live as good a Catholic life as I can, but this I cannot do. It is against my religion. I won't speak of it ever again, now get out of my room, just get out."

It wasn't long before I was kicked out of my lodgings again. Many times over the next few months and years I was arrested for being drunk and disorderly, and spent uncomfortable nights in the cells, waking up stinking of my own urine and vomit. Many times as well, I was left homeless, sleeping on the streets, collapsing drunk in alleyways. It was a wonder that I was never murdered! I must've had a Guardian Angel up there keeping an eye on me, and though I was hell bent on self-destruction, I somehow survived.

I had no money, it was all spent in the pubs, and so I fell into shoplifting for food, and clothing. Inevitably, I was caught and spent time in prison. I think by this stage I'd lost all hope. I had no faith in myself nor anyone around me. I stopped washing and cleaning my clothes, and I knew people called me a 'bag lady' or a 'down-and-out', and I didn't care. By 1967 I had no contact with any of my children, and I had sunk as low as a person could go into the mire of poverty and drunkenness.

By June 1971, I had been admitted several times into Birmingham General Hospital and was known as being an alcoholic. I don't remember how I did it, but somehow I'd had a bad fall and fractured the bone in my thigh. For eight long weeks I was an inpatient. When I was finally discharged, I went straight back to my usual begging spot, at the bottom of the ramp by New Street Station, to get the few pence I needed to buy Barley Wine, or if not, the cheapest cider. Decimal Day earlier in February had changed the currency from shillings to pounds and pence, yet all this passed me by. All I wanted each day was to get enough to go and spend the evening sipping my bottles as I sat on the benches near St Michael's Roman Catholic Church near the Bull Ring. I never went inside anymore, I didn't deserve to; I felt unworthy of setting foot inside a holy place. I didn't even go in any more to light a candle, one for each of my children, like I used to. But I was happy enough, sitting there in the lukewarm sunshine as day turned to night. I very often slept there as well, figuring that harm couldn't come to me so near a church.

Each morning the kind man with the hot potato stall in New

Street would give me a free spud for breakfast. I often told him that I'd given my Little Phyllis hot potatoes for breakfast and he'd nod and smile at me. It was a small glimmer of human kindness and I appreciated it.

A few months later, I found a derelict house in Heath Street, a dilapidated part of the city, and moved in. It was shelter at least.

One sunny day in June 1973, as I sat in my armchair, looking out at people passing by in the street, I suddenly decided to write a letter to the Mother Superior Sister Bernadette at Father Hudson's home. I don't know why I chose that moment, but it was as if the plan had been formulating for years and had crystallised into action. I scrabbled around to find a piece of paper and a pen, and sat for a long time wondering what to write. My mind was blank. How could I describe the last 16 years since Phyllis and I had been parted? How could I communicate the sense of loss that filled me to the brim? How could I say that I'd never spent a day without thinking of her? That she was the child I'd bonded with the most, the one I had with the only man I'd ever loved and who I missed like a part of me was gone? The last thing I had heard about her was that she had been put up for adoption. But what if she hadn't? What if she needed me, or just wanted to know who I was, and didn't know where to find me? What could I possibly say to make her want to see me?

I didn't know where to start. I got up and headed to The Shakespeare pub on the corner of Heath Street and Winson Street, and settled into 'my' seat next to a couple of drinking pals. Then the strangest thing happened. Two girls ran past. I barely noticed them, but suddenly I heard one of the girl's shout as clear as anything: "Come on Phyllis, your mum will be wondering where you are". My head was thick with drink, as usual, but the name penetrated into my soul. I looked up, trying to focus on the teenage girls, their blonde hair in ponytails, disappearing up Heath Street.

Was that a sign from God? Would I see my daughter again? Would I send that letter and find she hadn't been adopted after all and she was looking for me? That word 'Phyllis' was so clear, so bright, that I crossed myself, stunned everyone by refusing another drink and headed home to write that letter to the orphanage where I'd left my daughter.

CHAPTER 19
THINKING OF MY LITTLE PHYLLIS
June 1973 to November 9, 1981

June 1973

Dear Mother Superior,

A daughter of mine was placed at the orphanage hastily. Her name was Phyllis. Can you please tell me of her whereabouts as I am now assured of a better life and would like to have her back. My girl will be 17 years old now, a real lady.

Yours truly,

Bridget Ryan

I stared down at my handwriting, shaky like a young child's. There seemed so much more I wanted to say. I wanted to write that I had regretted giving up Little Phyllis every single day of the 16 years and three months since I let her go. I wanted to write that she was the pearl of my heart, and I ached for her. I wanted to tell the home that they should never have taken her in, and that she'd have been better off with me, though I knew that was wishful thinking.

I saw my life as 'better' because I had a roof over my head, but I saw what the drink had done to me each time I looked in my mirror. I was only 44 years old but my hair was matted, my teeth rotten, and I was avoided by all but the down-and-outs. My persona as Tipperary Mary was my outward appearance, yet it hid the pain I'd carried since a child. Now, I wanted to make amends, to see my beloved daughter, even if just for one visit. I wanted to know she was cared for and I wanted her to know me, the real me, not the 'crazy' lady who still begged at New Street Station each day for money for cider.

I was a mother, and I loved Phyllis with all my heart. She reminded me so much of my dear sister Philomena and, of course, I'd kept her for nine months. Yet I knew that asking after her might not bring me the news I craved. She might not want to see me.

She might turn away from me in disgust. She might have no interest in her Irish roots. She might love her adopted mother more than she ever could love me – and who could blame her? The thoughts swirled and collided in my mind.

That night in bed I tossed and turned, my head filled with worries and questions, unsure if sending the letter was the right move or not. It might upset Phyllis to know I was trying to find her. She might be settled and happy, and what I was about to do might unsettle her. She might be cross at me for leaving. She might hate me. Was I doing the right thing? I decided to pray about it, asking God for a sign that it was the right thing to do.

I barely slept. As I tossed and turned, I wondered if I could have done anything differently to save the mess my life had become. Perhaps if I had prayed harder when I was young; if I hadn't told Robert about me and Bill going away together; if I hadn't been so bold to the nuns in Roscrea so they sent me away from Kieran; if I had worked harder to make them believe the evil Robert had inflicted on me; if I had accepted help with Phyllis. If, above all, I had been able to resist the drink, then maybe I would have stood a chance. The one thing I knew I couldn't have differently was to fall in love with Bill, despite all the heartache and despair it caused me. It would be like telling me not to breathe – as long as I had breath in my body I would love the man. I knew I had done a lot that was wrong, but there was still a chance to put something right.

The next morning I woke up after finally dropping off just before dawn. It was a warm day, and I woke up lit by a shaft of sunlight across my crumpled bed. It was a hopeful sign surely, perhaps that was the sign I'd asked for? Before I knew it I'd dressed, queued in the post office for a stamp, and was standing at the post box, the envelope in my hand. As I let go of it I felt my heart unfurl, and with a contented smile I ambled home. I had done the right thing and who knows, for once things might just go my way.

When the reply came, barely a week later, I could hardly open the letter, my hands were trembling so much. I scanned the page, then read it slowly. There wasn't much to take in. My heart thumped wildly.

Dear Miss Ryan,
Thank you for your letter. Phyllis was adopted 13 years ago. She is happily settled and my Society has not heard of her in that time, of course in adoption no news is good news.
Yours Sincerely,
Sister Bernadette *(Mother Superior)*

I scrunched up that letter, tearing it into shreds. Tears streamed down my face, though at least I had my answer. The years of wondering what had happened to her, hoping that she was loved and that she now lived with a nice respectable, family were over. She had been adopted and could now be living anywhere, even another country for all I knew. I had to trust that she was happy and that her carers were well-chosen by the orphanage.

Yet despite this news, the loss of my daughter suddenly felt as fresh as the day I left her, perhaps because I knew now that I would never see her again.

Everyone I loved had been lost to me; Philomena, Mam, my brother Jimmie, Bill and my children. I was alone, completely alone with my grief, and there was only one thing left I could do to take away the horror, and that was to head for the next drink.

My drinking became worse, if that was possible. I barely knew a sober day after that letter arrived. My life, which was chaotic at the best of times, descended into full-blown madness.

Two years later, I was brought into the A&E department of Dudley Hospital at 2am by the police following a drunken brawl.

"Get off me. I'm fine, get your filthy hands off me!" I screeched, kicking out at the two policemen who held me by the arms. "I don't need no hospital. Let go of me!"

"Calm down Tipperary Mary, we can't let you go, you've injured yourself. If you carry on screaming and shouting we'll have to arrest you." Both policemen knew me, I was an infamous figure in the area now, a figure of pity and ridicule.

"Do what ye like with me, I don't care, so I don't! That man was askin' for it – he didn't even ask me which drink I wanted."

I had started a brawl in the early hours during a lock-in, as I'd poured the contents of my glass over the head of the man who'd bought it for me. Most nights someone would buy me a pint of bitter so I'd stay quiet, sitting in the corner all alone. That night, I took exception to the fact that the man, who coincidentally was also from Tipperary, hadn't asked me what I wanted before he ordered my drink. I thought that was a cheek, never mind the fact I wasn't buying it! When the drink took hold and my mood grew dark I could argue with my own shadow.

"He doesn't know how to treat a lady," I declared, squirming to free myself from the policemen's grip.

"A lady? Listen to yourself with airs and graces? Well, she's a feisty one, I'll give her that," laughed one of the coppers.

"Now then Miss Ryan, what's the problem?" asked the staff nurse who'd been assigned to me. She seemed quite bossy and had a stern look on her plain face.

"Ahem, now these here policemen have caught me and won't let me go. I don't mean anyone any harm," I said pathetically as one of the men coughed with restrained incredulity.

"Now, Miss Ryan, you can't come in here and start shouting the place down," said the staff nurse.

"We've got some very sick patients in here this evening so I need you to calm down so we can have a look at that cut on your head."

I felt my forehead. It was sticky with blood. I had no idea how the injury had got there, and no recollection of the evening much beyond pouring that drink over the poor man's head. This stopped my protests. I knew I could spoil for a fight when I was drunk and obviously this one had turned nasty. So at this point I sheepishly apologised to the policemen, who let me go, at last.

"Now let's clean up your cut and get you settled. We'll most likely keep you in tonight, keep an eye on you and give you a nice breakfast in the morning, how does that sound?" asked the nurse as she collected her swabs and antiseptic wipes, ready to clean me up.

"It looks like it's a glass that's cut you. It must've been one hell of a pub fight, Bridget," she tutted. I nodded, it must have been but I didn't remember too much about it.

I must have passed out as the next thing I knew it was morning. I had been kept in overnight, covered with a blanket in the recovery position in a cubicle close to the nurse's station so they could keep an eye on me. I woke up the next day with a pounding head but feeling much more like my old self, when I heard a passing nurse say: "That's Bridget Ryan, she's a well-known alcoholic and lives in the area…" I was stung into shouting back: "Ye feckin' do-gooders!" My voice stopped them in their tracks outside my cubicle.

"I'm not a feckin' alcoholic, I only drink a few Barley wines. That bastard hit me with a glass and now my feckin' head is bleeding. Isn't anyone going to help me PLEASE!" I bellowed.

A young nurse put her head round the curtain. She had lovely blonde hair and I noticed her piercing blue eyes straight away. Something about her made me suddenly stop struggling.

"Now then Bridget, let me give you a wash and smarten you up a bit. You could do with a new nightie and a once-over with a flannel and some soap!" she said with a smile in her voice.

I stared back at her, all the while thinking this nurse reminded me of someone, she looked so familiar.

"What's your name?" I said, woozy now from the effects of the hangover and injury.

"My name is Nurse Price, but you can call me Phyllis."

At that I almost choked. "Phyllis, you say? Phyllis. My daughter was called Phyllis…." I wanted to say more but my head started hurting and everything went hazy again.

"That's nice, Bridget, now please lie back and let me do my job, I'll be as gentle as I can. You look like you've been through 10 rounds with Mohammed Ali!"

I smiled back at her. There was something about this nurse that made me feel instantly peaceful.

She washed me down, being careful with me and helped me wiggle out of my dirty clothes and into a freshly cleaned nightdress. I couldn't remember the last time someone had looked after me like that. It calmed me down instantly, and made me grateful to the point of crying. When she'd finished, I grabbed for her hand, and she stood there for a good while and just held it as I squeezed my eyes shut to stop the tears coming.

That nurse named Phyllis, like my daughter, spoke to me so gently that day, dressing my wound and finally discharging me with a sweet smile. Even though my life continued to be difficult, I never forgot that magical moment of tenderness in the hospital, and the nurse who looked after me with such love and kindness.

***

Six years later, I was sitting in my armchair, looking out of the window watching the world go by. I lived in Runcorn Road in Balsall Heath, in a lodging owned by Moseley Housing Association. A man called Timmy, whom I'd met in a pub, was the tenant and he'd let me stay out of pity, saying I could be his 'housekeeper'. I don't suppose Timmy was actually allowed to let me stay but in the end I stayed for 11 years.

Timmy was also a drinker, like me, which meant we had one thing in common at least – but I kept out of his way as much as possible.

I caught a glimpse of my battered swollen face, congealed blood in my hair as I glanced into the mirror. My head was hurting from a fall I'd had the previous day.

Earlier, I discovered a can of Timmy's extra-strong lager, which he always hid under his bed. I opened it and took a swig. I sat for a while, reflecting on how things had gone so badly wrong for me in my life. Maybe I didn't always get things right, especially with the drink, but I didn't know any other way of coping with the memories that came back to haunt me.

I knew why I drank. It was the only peace I could find. A way to block out the trauma of my past; the shock of seeing my stepfather swinging from his own belt, the upset of my mammy dying in my arms and the years I'd sacrificed staying home from school to care for her, losing my brother Jimmie and then little Philomena whisked away to become a Conroy and cutting all contact with me - though I loved her dearly. Then on top of all that, the terrible ordeal at the hands of my own brother Robert, bearing his child and being punished for the wickedness wrought upon me. I drank to kill the pain of giving up Kieran, of being bullied by those nuns at Roscrea, at the unfairness of being sectioned and placed in a mental hospital just for speaking the truth. Then Bill, my beloved Bill, left me when I was three months pregnant with our child, who I tried to be a good mammy to, but the odds were stacked against me. I tried – and failed, and I drank to block the pain of handing her over, too.

My 'Little Phyllis' came into my mind. I could still picture her cherubic little face so clearly, the look of confusion, then upset as she was carried out of my arms. I hoped one day she'd forgive me for giving her up, as I couldn't forgive myself. I wondered in those quiet moments, as I sat in my chair in November, 1981, if she'd got married, whether I was a grand-mother? I thought of Kieran, wondering where he was in the world right now and whether he was happy. I thought of all my children, what might have been if I had been able to cope. Where were they all now? Did they ever think of me, their birth mother? Or was my face a blur from childhood, long-forgotten as they grew into the people they had become?

I'd never have answers to my questions, I accepted that now. Phyllis's little face came into my mind's eye and I smiled again. I'd looked after her for nine whole months. I'd tried my hardest for my daughter, and I hoped somehow she'd know that. I sent her a small prayer, whispered to no-one but myself and God.

"Please God, please keep lookin' after my Littl' Phyllis. Please God she was adopted by a loving family, with money in their purse and good prospects for her. Please God keep her safe, and wherever she is, tell her I love her."

Just then there was a knock at the door. I eased myself up and out of the chair, wondering who was calling. I wasn't expecting anyone. I opened the door. Standing in front of me was a young district nurse. The smiling blonde woman with startlingly blue eyes, asked softly: "Are you Bridget? May I come inside?"

A SONG FOR BRIDGET

EPILOGUE

My mother 'Tipperary Mary' did have my best interests at heart when she left me at the orphanage at the age of nine months. I found out many years later that when she brought me in, I was clean, podgy and well-cared for, in stark contrast to her own terrible, neglected state.

My mum had bathed me, changed my clothes and cradled me in her arms, yet she had to walk away, hoping that one day we might be reunited.

I eventually knocked on her front door two days before her 53rd birthday. She was clearly a damaged soul. It was written in the scars and lines that formed her face, the tattered hair, the unwashed clothes, all remnants of the heartache and abuse she'd suffered over the years. There was something familiar about her face and I realised that I had met her once before. Fate had first brought us together in a Birmingham hospital six years earlier, when, as a trainee nurse, I tended to my mother's wounds after she had been brought into the A&E department following a drunken brawl. At the time, neither of us knew who the other was but, as strangers, we seemed to have an ease with one another, an understanding of sorts. Perhaps it was that meeting that quietly inspired me to start looking for my birth mum a few years later at the age of 23.

While I recognised the woman before me as I stood on her doorstep in November 1981, she had no clue who I was and I kept it that way. It was my turn to care for her now and I did for nine years, never telling her who I really was, though my instincts told me she knew somewhere deep down inside herself. I bathed her, changed her clothing and cradled her in my arms to protect her from harm, just as she had done for me for the first nine months of my life.

I listened to her stories for hours on end. They were often interspersed with bizarre asides that trailed off into nonsense, but eventually I managed to piece together the whole story of her life, the story that makes up this book, the prequel to my own memoir Finding Tipperary Mary.

I hope that in writing this story (adding in everything I have learned), charting my mother's harrowing life, I will understand the forces that shaped her, that made her the tragic figure she became. I want this book, her book, to prove her life was not in vain and in telling her story, she will never be forgotten.

I also hope that my mother's struggles will help others to understand that behind any addiction to alcohol or drugs, there is emotional and psychological pain or trauma. They are damaged people who deserve our support and understanding, not our condemnation. And no one could have endured what my mum did in her early life without being damaged profoundly. Mum was spared the pain of seeing her son Billy die from a heroin overdose at just 30 years old. They say addiction is a family disease – and tragically, Billy proved just that.

When I first visited my mum as a district nurse on that fateful day in November 1981, she believed I was her nurse who cared for her, which I was, but I admit I did it unofficially in order to get to know her without trespassing on her feelings and her life.

I never knew if she was strong enough to handle the truth, that the woman tending her bruises, was, in fact, her long-lost daughter. Nor if my own young family could handle the chaos of having 'Tipperary Mary' in their everyday lives. That's why I never told her.

Strangely, over those years we did develop a mother-daughter relationship of a sort. Surely part of loving someone is tolerating them for who they really are, and Bridget demanded a lot of tolerance, which I was happy to give.

I recall one afternoon in the early days of me visiting mum, she told me to "clear off" (or words to that effect!) very aggressively. So I did. I hurried to my car feeling close to tears. As I took a few deep breaths to compose myself, I suddenly saw my mum peeking out of her window, staring at me, as I looked at her tired face, I saw the exhaustion and confusion etched into her features, and she suddenly shouted: "Are ye feckin' coming next week?"

I called back: "Do you want me to come and see you?" She looked away and then shouted: "Ach, I wouldn't feckin' ask ye if I didn't want ye to come!"

I knew by then that was the best invitation I was going to get and I told her I'd be back, a smile playing about my lips. She was hard work. Her defences were always up, and she rarely allowed any softness in her words or deeds, but there was also something sad and pathetic about her. Inside her was a little girl who had never been loved properly, and even though I barely knew her, I could sense that from the start.

Her response was unexpected. She smiled, which was something she rarely did. I knew then that she wanted me to continue visiting her. I drove away and realised I loved her as my mother, and would never stop visiting her.

In her latter years, when she was living with dementia, I visited her regularly at the home she then lived in. In February 2003 she died, leaving me mourning the mother who never knew her daughter. Bridget was a dysfunctional mother, a drunk and a very damaged woman, but she was my mum. She was the last piece of my own jigsaw.

Years later when I travelled to Templemore in Southern Ireland to learn all I could about my mother's roots, I knew she was there with me. It was 2017 when I visited County Tipperary for the first time, and there I lit a candle for her in Sacred Heart Church in Templemore. It was as if I felt her presence, as I feel it still. Her life was a tangled web, and I don't know if I've uncovered all the strands of it, but I do know that this book, my tribute to Tipperary Mary, is a heartfelt attempt to understand her as a victim of circumstances out of her control.

History was cruel to unmarried mothers, and her life bears witness to this. The Catholic Church has so much to answer for. How many young women's lives were destroyed by forced adoption, by their young lovers disappearing, leaving them to fend alone, their babies taken, their lives changed and altered without kindness or understanding?

Much was done to you, mum, that was wrong, but you are at peace now, and this book is your legacy.

Mum, I know you're watching over me, and I love you.

Phyllis

x

ACKNOWLEDGEMENTS

To my three children Stuart, Hannah and Tom who never knew their grandmother growing up, but at least now they have a better understanding of her vulnerability.

I'm so grateful to my nursing profession, which enabled me to care for vulnerable adults. I couldn't have imagined when I started my career, that the most vulnerable person I would ever look after would be my own mum. But she welcomed me into her home and allowed me to spend precious time with her.

To Cathryn Kemp who managed to read through my research and waffle and told my Mum's story in such a sensitive and understanding way. And thanks to Editor Charlotte Cole for her hard work.

To the amazing Mirror Books team, especially Fergus McKenna, who was so supportive. A very special thank you goes to Jo Sollis who recognised that there was much more of my mum's story to be told and encouraged me to research further into her past, you really are a true professional.

A big thank you to Mel Sambells who has been so helpful and given much of her time to me, she truly is a lovely person.

To my 'Greek family' and friends in Kefalonia who have followed me on my journey and inspired me to continue with my writing!

Through writing my books I have met so many wonderful people who have shared their own heartbreaking stories with me. Some even knew my Mum when she was out and about in Birmingham – like Frank, the retired bus conductor, who often let my Mum off without paying her fare! Thanks to Margaret the retired midwife who worked at Gulson Hospital in Coventry and knew only too well how hard it was for unmarried mothers to keep their babies.

Finally, on a more personal level, I am grateful to writer Barbara Fisher, who continues to give me her support. Tom and Mary O'Rielly (my cousin and his wife) who are unfailing in their guidance and encouragement, and my close friends and cousins who understood my reasons for wanting to find out the truth about my past. Thank you all from the bottom of my heart.

Also by Mirror Books

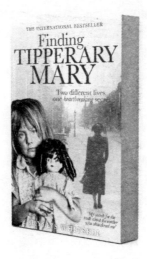

THE INTERNATIONAL BESTSELLER

Finding Tipperary Mary
Phyllis Whitsell

The astonishing real story of a daughter's search for her own past
and the desperate mother who gave her up for adoption.

Phyllis Whitsell began looking for her birth mother as a young
woman and although it was many years before she finally met her, their
lives had crossed on the journey without their knowledge.
When they both eventually sat together in the same room,
the circumstances were extraordinary, moving and
ultimately life-changing.

This is a daughter's personal account of the remarkable
relationship that grew from abandonment into love,
understanding and selfless care.

Mirror Books

Also by Mirror Books

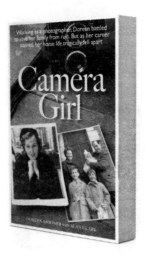

Camera Girl
Doreen Spooner with Alan Clark

The true story of a woman coping with a tragic end to the love of her life, alongside a daily fight to establish herself and support her children.

A moving and inspiring memoir of Doreen Spooner – a woman ahead of her time. Struggling to hold her head high through the disintegration of the family she loves through alcoholism, she began a career as Fleet Street's first female photographer.

While the passionate affair and family life she'd always dreamed of fell apart, Doreen walked into the frantic world of a national newspaper. Determined to save her family from crippling debt, her work captured the Swinging Sixties through political scandals, glamorous stars and cultural icons, while her homelife spiralled further out of control.

The two sides of this book take you through a touching and emotional love story, coupled with a hugely enjoyable portrait of post-war Britain.

Also by Mirror Books

1963 - A Slice of Bread and Jam
Tommy Rhattigan

Tommy lives at the heart of a large Irish family in derelict Hulme in Manchester, ruled by an abusive, alcoholic father and a negligent mother. Alongside his siblings he begs (or steals) a few pennies to bring home to avoid a beating, while looking for a little adventure of his own along the way.

His foul-mouthed and chaotic family may be deeply flawed, but amongst the violence, grinding poverty and distinct lack of hygiene and morality lies a strong sense of loyalty and, above all, survival.

During this single year – before his family implodes and his world changes for ever – Tommy almost falls foul of the welfare officers, nuns, police – and Myra Hindley and Ian Brady.

An adventurous, fun, dark and moving true story of the only life young Tommy knew.

Mirror Books